A Short History of Socialist Economic Thought

A Short History of Socialist Economic Thought

Gerd Hardach and Dieter Karras
in association with Ben Fine

Translated by James Wickham

St. Martin's Press   New York

English translation and edition
© 1978 Edward Arnold (Publishers) Ltd

Authorized translation from the German
Sozialistische Wirtschaftstheorie
© 1974 Wissenschaftliche Buchgesellschaft

First published in the United States of America in 1979
by St. Martin's Press

ISBN 0-312-72147-1 paperback
ISBN 0-312-72146-3 cloth

Cover illustration: *The proletariat getting free from the chains of capitalism,* Karl Marx and Friedrich Engels Musuem, Moscow. Courtesy of Novosti Press Agency.

Library of Congress Cataloging in Publication Data

Hardach, Gerd, 1941-
    A short history of socialist economic thought.

    Translation of Sozialistische Wirtschaftstheorie.
    Includes bibliographical references and indexes.
    1. Marxian economics — History. I. Karras,
Dieter, 1945-   joint author. II. Fine, Ben, joint
author. III. Title.
HB97.5.H3413   1979   335.4'09   78-21053
ISBN 0-312-72146-3
ISBN 0-312-72147-1 pbk.

june '80

Contents

Abbreviations

References to works by Marx, Engels and Lenin are to the following standard editions:

MECW Karl Marx and Frederick Engels, *Collected Works*, London, Lawrence and Wishart, 1975-.
MEW Karl Marx, Friedrich Engels: *Werke*, Berlin, Dietz, 1972.
MESW Karl Marx and Frederick Engels, *Selected Works in Three Volumes*, Moscow, Progress Publishers, 1969.
CW Lenin, *Collected Works*, Moscow, Progress Publishers, 1960-.

Page references to Marx's *Capital* are to the Moscow (Progress Publishers) edition; for *Capital* vol. 1 the corresponding pages in the new Penguin edition (translated by Ben Fowkes) are also indicated in brackets. References to Marx's *'Results of the Immediate Process of Production'* are to the translation published as an appendix to the Penquin edition of *Capital* vol. 1

References added by the translator are indicated by square brackets.

Authors' Introduction

This study has three aims: first, to trace the origins and the development of socialist economic thought; secondly, to show the specific preconditions for the various theories, and thirdly to develop starting points for criticism.

As far as the selection of material is concerned, socialism here means primarily the opposition to capitalism of an alternative conception of society. This definition determines the historical limits of the study: we have only discussed theories which developed out of criticism both of the capitalist economy and the capitalist social order and of the economic theories which justified capitalist economic conditions. Concretely, this means that only with the onset of the industrial revolution in England at the end of the eighteenth century did the preconditions exist for a critique of capitalist forms of production. Here for the first time the principles of economic liberalism, individual competition and the separation of wage labour and capital began to operate across society as a whole; here for the first time these principles began to find their advocates among the bourgeois economists. Once this occurred there began to develop, so to speak as a polar opposite, conceptions of cooperation (with or without state participation), and proposals for the socializaton of the means of production as a way of overcoming exploitation and the search for profit.

Socialist economics is therefore primarily the critique of capitalism and the critique of (bourgeois) political economy. Certainly, the early socialists did use their critique of bourgeois society to develop detailed utopias, while the general determinants of the future socialist society were worked out in the period of scientific socialism. However, only after 1917 did the second area of socialist economics really develop, namely the political economy of socialism as the analysis of the economic laws of the transitional society.

Socialist economics therefore divides clearly into two parts, each with different objects and each with different methods. We have restricted ourselves to a discussion of the first part, socialist theories of capitalism. We have been concerned to present socialist economics through a discussion of its central problems, even when this has meant sacrificing a complete listing of all the authors who had any connection with the area.

After this study was started the authors' paths became geographically separated, and this led to our cooperation not being as close as was originally planned. Chapters 1 and 2 were prepared largely by Dieter Karras, Chapters 3 and 4 by Gerd Hardach, but the basic conception and the final version remain the result of joint work.

This English edition has been augmented by a chapter on recent developments in Marxist economic theory prepared by Ben Fine, and appearing as Chapter 5.

Translator's Introduction

This book is an introduction to socialist economic thought, largely but not exclusively to Marxist economic thought. The importance of economics for socialist thinkers pre-dates Marx: as Hardach and Karras make clear, the early socialists too considered that the key to understanding society lay in its economic basis. However, as I shall attempt to show in this introduction, going to the economic basis means challenging conventional notions of what economics are about, ideas, it should be admitted, which are prevalent within Marxism itself.

For Hardach and Karras Marx's work is distinguished by its method, yet they fail to make clear that because Marx's concepts are different, so too is his object of study. It is here, and not in the method per se, that lies the distinctiveness and the radicalness of Marx's work.

It is often claimed that Marxism is different to 'bourgeois' social thought because it is linked explicitly to socialist political action. Such a view ultimately reduces the validity of theory to some existential *prise de position*, condemning theory to be the mere justification of an existing political practice. At its worst, this argument judges all theories in terms of their political consequences, with the obvious result that is impossible ever to assess the political position from which the judgement is itself being made. One of the great merits of this study is that since Hardach and Karras tackle theory as theory, they do not fall into this trap.

Alternatively, it is sometimes argued that Marxism is about 'totality' as opposed to the fragmentation of conventional academic disciplines.[1] Hardach and Karras for example claim that Marx's own investigation 'aimed to understand society as a whole'.[2] Such a position entails two problems. First, it involves an understanding of the relationship between different areas of society in terms of what Althusser has termed 'an expressive totality' – the idea that distinctive areas all express or reflect some common inner principle (usually claimed to be the economy). The consequence of this reductionism is that anything which does not fit into this schema has to be treated as an aberration. Secondly, the apparent radicalism of the demand for an all-embracing theory actually masks the radical nature of Marx's challenge to bourgeois social thought, for it becomes impossible to see that the Marxist concepts of economics and politics are themselves different to what the academic disciplines of economics and political science study, while the concept of 'society' is a concept the validity of which Marxism actually challenges.[3] While space prevents me from demonstrating this last point here, it is implied in the difference between bourgeois and Marxist economics, a difference which can perhaps be formulated in the difference between the (bourgeois) concept of economics and the (Marxist) concept of the economic, as designating two different objects.

At their most general level Marx's economic concepts do not apply only to capitalism. The most abstract section of *Capital* (and hence the real beginning of the book) is not the famous analysis of the 'commodity form' in Part I,[4] but the analysis of the labour process, for there Marx initially treats the labour process 'independently of the particular form it assumes under given social conditions'.[5] It is only after he has analysed the three basic elements of the labour process (the object of labour, the means of labour, the activity of labouring) that Marx then analyses the labour process within capitalism. However, moving directly from the analysis of the labour process in general to the analysis of the labour process in capitalism (as Marx himself does here) is illegitimate. Before this can be done the general nature of production – as opposed to that of the labour process per se – has to be established, and this involves locating the basis of any form of class exploitation.

Even in a classless society, production presupposes people who do not directly work, since there will always be those who cannot directly produce: children, old people, the temporarily ill, etc.[6] Hence production – i.e. the economic level itself – involves (1) the labourer – the person who actually carries out the activity of work; (2) the means of production – i.e. both the object and the means of labour, and finally (3) the non-labourer – those who do not produce. As Balibar points out,[7] any mode of production involves two relationships between these three elements, what he terms the 'property connexion' and the 'real or material appropriation connexion'.[8] The former can be considered as what is traditionally called the relations of production, that is to say, those relationships which determine the power to dispose of the results of production, while the latter is equivalent to the forces of production, i.e. the relationships which determine the immediate organization of production.

It is from the relations of production that classes are derived: classes exist when the means of production are owned by a distinct group of non-labourers. Classes, therefore, are not unique to capitalism. Thus in the feudal mode of production, although the direct producer or labourer 'possesses' the means of production, since he himself actually directs and controls immediate production, the results of this production are distributed through his relationship to the feudal lord who appropriates a proportion of the total production for his own use. To quote Althusser:

> The production relation is, says Marx, a relation of distribution: it distributes men among classes at the same time and according as it attributes the means of

production to a class. The classes are born out of the antagonism in this distribution which is also an attribution.[9]

Any class mode of production then involves the expropriation of the immediate producers, since they do not own the means of production. However, in the capitalist mode of production the producers are not only expropriated, they are also dispossessed as well, since they have no control over the direct organization of production. We can now rejoin Marx's argument as he moves to the analysis of the capitalist labour process:

> The labour process, turned into the process by which the capitalist consumes labour-power, exhibits two characteristic phenomena. First, the labourer works under the control of the capitalist to whom his labour belongs [i.e. the capitalist supervises and directs the work: while it occurs under the control of the capitalist, it is also impossible without him – JW]. Secondly, the product is the property of the capitalist and not that of the labourer, its immediate producer [i.e. it is the capitalist who decides what is to be produced and to what purpose – JW].[10]

It turns out therefore that the basis of society – the economic – is not outside of society at all. Rather than being some extra-social 'material' basis, the economic in any mode of production is defined by these two relationships (relations and forces of production) which are in both cases relationships between people and between people and things. Nonetheless, these relationships are material in that they cannot be reduced to purely social relationships in the conventional sense. As Louis Althusser has recently expressed it.:

> It is one of the greatest possible theoretical mystifications that you can imagine to think that social relations can be reduced to relations between men, or even between groups of men: because this is to suppose that social relations are relations which only involve men, whereas actually they also involve things, the means of production, derived from material nature.[11]

The notion of the 'basis' therefore can be rather misleading if it is taken as involving some extra-social area from which 'society' is to be explained. It is also misleading a second sense: it can mask the fact that class struggle is internal to the economic, and not just derived from the 'the economy'. In any class mode of production, the material production of 'use values' is at the same time a struggle for the appropriation of surplus labour from which the dominant class lives. Because the Marxist theory of the economic starts from production itself, it necessarily insists that the relations it studies are inherently relations of domination and exploitation. Here we can notice the difference to the subject matter of conventional (bourgeois) economics, which defines question of power and conflict as purely social and consequently assigns such questions to the sociologists for study. The sociologists, in turn, obediently define social relations as purely 'social' in the way that Althusser criticizes. Consequently, sociology's discussion of power and conflict is necessarily idealist, treating individuals as pre-existing, never asking how such individuals produce and hence reproduce themselves materially. In a mutual conspiracy of mystification, bourgeois sociology and bourgeois economics define away material exploitation and material conflict.

The economic therefore itself includes class struggle. This economic class struggle is not just a question of trade union organizations or even 'spontaneous' and uninstitutionalized wage demands: this is to confuse the organizational forms within which the struggle sometimes occurs, with the actual struggle itself, a struggle which is an ever present and everyday reality in any class mode of production, a struggle which is at the core of the Marxist concept of the economic.

From this understanding of the economic three important consequences follow: the rejection of technicism, the rejection of teleology, and paradoxically, the importance of the political.

By 'technicism' I mean an understanding of the forces of production as developing according to their own internal logic. Within Marxism such an idea has a long history, being present to some extent in Marx's own work and being conceptually identical to the bourgeois notion of the inevitability of 'technological progress'. However, once we insist that capitalist production necessarily involves both exploitation (i.e. the extraction of surplus labour in the form of surplus value) and domination (i.e. control by some people of other people), then the actual organization of production is in no way neutral. The way in which a factory is physically laid out, the construction of the machines, let alone the forms of organization of the workers and the wage structure, all can be seen as necessarily not what they are claimed to be, the scientifically best and most efficient way to produce a particular product, but rather the way a particular product is produced within a particular form of capitalism. Changes in machinery and in the organization of work thus become just as much part of the class struggle as conflicts over wages or conditions, 'technological innovation' is part of the continual struggle by the capitalist class not simply to make profits, but also, and just as importantly, to retain control within the production process.[12] The accumulation of capital, with its accompanying centralization and concentration, is equally not an objective economic law, but the form of the economic class struggle within the capitalist mode of production. Given this, it is clear that there is no such thing as a logic of technology outside the social relations (relations in the Marxist and materialist sense) within which technology is embedded. Once again, there is no material basis which drives social development forward from the outside.

From the rejection of technicism follows the rejection of teleology, the idea that history has a logical end (socialism) towards which it is inevitably progressing. Marxist teleology stands or falls within the notion of the autonomous development of the forces of production. Once the economic is defined as including class struggle then, as we have seen, the forces of production have no autonomous development. This can be expressed in the formula of the domination of the relations of production over the forces of production: it is the relations of production which define specific classes and permit the development of specific 'technologies'. Thus, quite against many traditional Marxist accounts, it is the relations of production, not the forces of production, which change first. Captialist industrial production, for example, required as a necessary precondition the prior establishment of capitalist relations of production, that is of unfettered private ownership of wealth on the one hand, and the creation of a class of individuals with no way of maintaining themselves except by working for a wage on the other.[13]

Traditionally Marxists have been embarrassed that socialist revolution has occurred not in the advanced capitalist countries of the West, but in areas where capitalism had only begun to penetrate (Russia, China). Such an understanding of history is incredibly Euro-centred, comfortingly locating historical progress always in the same geographical and cultural space. Marx himself frequently says that socialism results from the contradiction between the development of the forces of production and the continuation of the same relations of production and thus implies that it is precisely the most advanced forms of capitalism which lead to socialism. Nonetheless, Marx's own concepts show that this is not the case: socialism, as surely the Chinese revolution has demonstrated, results not from the development of the forces of production, but purely and simply from the transformation of the relations of production through class struggle.

Such a transformation however is not achieved by economic but by political class struggle. The economic cannot exist by itself, but has 'conditions of existence', conditions which are ideological and (in a class mode of production) political. That is to say, relations of production which are relations of exploitation (i.e. class relations) have to be secured by a state as the area where class power is organized.[14] The political, as above all Poulantzas[15] has made clear, refers to the state; hence politics is that form of class struggle which has as its objective the state itself. Especially in the capitalist mode of production, the political processes of of class domination cannot be reduced to mere economic processes[16] – political concepts are distinct from economic concepts even within Marxism, Marxism is not a political economy in the sense of a merger of economics and politics.

The Marxist concept of the political is quite distinct from bourgeois notions of politics, and the reason lies in the Marxist theory of the state. Following Gramsci, many Marxist writers argue that the state has to be understood as including institutions which are legally not part of the state at all (e.g. the Church, the media). However, more is involved than the question of the institutional area which is to be defined as 'the state'. In differing ways, writers such as Hirsch and Poulantzas show that the state is not an institution but a class relationship.[17] The consequence is that although in one sense, as we have just seen, the Marxist concept of the political covers a wider area than the bourgeois concept of politics, in a second sense it is much narrower. Not only does the Marxist concept mean that the political is specific to class modes of production, it also quite clearly means that hierarchy is not in itself inherently political.

To confuse hierarchy and the political is to understand social relations in sociological and not in Marxist terms, for power and domination are now related solely to relationships between people. The consequence is two mistakes which were particularly clear in the practice of the radical student movement of the 1960s. First, it is ignored that in a class society it is precisely the state which actually maintains and secures 'hierarchy', and that consequently it is the state which must be the ultimate reference point for any socialist strategy. Secondly, and rather paradoxically, once 'everything' is claimed to be political, then the specific nature of the different levels of struggle is occluded, and it even becomes possible to deny that they exist. For example, while I have argued that the economic itself includes class struggle, it has often been fashionable to argue that the struggle over 'mere' wages is unimportant and possibly even reactionary. Once there is no specific concept of the political, then it becomes possible to use the astounding discovery that trade unions do not usually make revolutions to claim that trade union conflict is merely 'part of the system'.

Equally, the obsession with hierarchy makes it easy to ignore the importance of theoretical production and ideological struggle, for knowledge becomes merely part of action or 'praxis'. By contrast, once the specific nature of the political is established, then the importance of ideology as an area both of struggle and of analysis becomes clear. Indeed, although the problem of ideology cannot be discussed here, it is clear that there is an analogous 'displacement' to that we have located in the case of economics and the economic – the Marxist concept of ideology is very distinct from the idealist notion of 'cultural values'.[18]

At the economic, political and ideological levels, Marxist theory differs from the bourgeois theory in two ways: it involves a distinctive object and it is centred on class struggle. However, each level remains distinct and each level involves its own concepts. To treat Marxist theory as largely economic, as Hardach and Karras do, is therefore unacceptable. In particular, it means that any concrete situation can only be analysed in terms of economic concepts plus the oft appealed to 'particular social and historical conditions'. Yet since the possibility of analysing these conditions in theoretically based terms is denied by the reduction of Marxism to the economic level, they must be treated in an ad hoc manner, a manner which is therefore always in danger of taking over bourgeois definitions and concepts. Nonetheless, the production of Marxist political and ideological concepts depends upon the existence of Marxist economic concepts, and to this material and theoretical economic basis Hardach and Karras provide an invaluable introduction.

NOTES

1 Cf. for example the work of George Lukacs, notably 'Reification and the Consciousness of the Proletariat' in his *History and Class Consciousness* (London, 1971).
2 P. 16 of this study.
3 Cf. G. Stedman Jones, 'From historical sociology to theoretical history' *BJS* 27:3 (September 1976), pp 295–306.
4 Cf. p. 18 below.
5 *Capital* vol 1, 177 (283).
6 Cf. Marx, *Critique of the Gotha Programme*, MESW, 3, 16.
7 L. Althusser & E. Balibar, *Reading Capital*, London, 1970, p. 215.
8 Ibid.
9 L. Althusser, *Essays in Self Criticism*, London, 1976, p. 202.
10 K. Marx, *Capital* vol 1, 184–5 (291–2).
11 Althusser, *op. cit.*, pp 201–202.
12 Cf. especially H. Braverman, *Labor and Monopoly Capital*, (New York and London, 1976).
13 Cf. Marx's analysis of 'primitive accumulation' in *Capital* vol 1, 713ff (873ff), also recent work by historians: I. Wallerstein, *The Modern World-System: Capitalist Agriculture and the Origins of the European World Economy in the Sixteenth Century* (New York and London, 1974); C. Tilly, 'Food Supply and Public Order in Early Modern Europe' in C. Tilly, (ed.), *The Formation of National States in Western Europe* (Princeton, 1975), especially pp. 414ff.
14 Cf. B. Hindess and P. Hirst, *Pre-Capitalist Modes of Production* (London, 1975), p 29.
15 N. Poulantzas, *Political Power and Social Classes* (London, 1973), especially ch. 1.
16 Cf. J. Hirsch, 'Bemerkungen zum theoretischen Ansatz einer Analyse des buergerlichen Staates' (University of Frankfurt, MS 1976; partly translated as 'Remarks on the Theoretical Analysis of the Bourgeois State' (Trinity College Dublin, Department of Sociology, MS, 1977).
17 While Poulantzas in particular is quite explicit in his rejection of any institutional definition of the state (Poulantzas, *op. cit.*, p. 115n), his commitment to 'Leninism' prevents him from drawing the consequence which follows for political organization – namely that the cadre political party cannot be the sole organization through which socialist transformation is achieved. cf J. Wickham, 'Nicos Poulantzas and the Dilemmas of Leninism' (Trinity College Dublin, Department of Sociology, MS, 1977).
18 Cf. R. Coward & J. Ellis, *Language and Materialism* (forthcoming), ch. 5.

A Short History of Socialist Economic Thought

I

THE CRITIQUE OF CAPITALISM AND PERSPECTIVES OF SOCIALIST SOCIETY BEFORE MARX

In the second half of the eighteenth century the industrial revolution began to spread, first in Britain and then later on the Continent, bringing with it a rapid development of the forces of production. This situation, it was widely believed, would soon bring about an improvement in the living conditions of *all* social classes.

This optimism at first did not seem unrealistic, but it soon proved to be illusory. The capitalist mode of production certainly increased the total wealth of society as a whole, but at the same time there arose a continually increasing class of wage workers, workers who had only their labour power to sell and whose wages were scarcely above subsistence level. This contradiction of wealth and poverty soon found its theorectical justification. For the leading economists of Britain, Thomas Robert MALTHUS (1766–1834) and David RICARDO (1772–1823) and of France, Jean-Baptiste SAY (1767–1832), the misery of the lower classes corresponded to a law of nature, indeed for them such misery was the precondition of economic development: in their eyes poverty was the stimulus to production. However, as the contradiction persisted that material need now coexisted with social wealth, and as economic theorists provided explanations for this situation, so too arose the first critical voices. This critique of the allegedly natural nature of poverty was initially expressed only by isolated individuals and remained without any great effects. However, as the misery of the lower classes became an ever more urgent social problem and as a solution remained non-existent, so ever wider circles were drawn into critical opposition to capitalism.

As capitalism spread continuously into all areas of economic life, and while the resulting exploitation and emiseration fuelled doubts as to the benefits of the new mode of production, many economic proposals for improving the workers' situation increasingly took on a socialist character. This socialism manifested itself in that the economic individualism of capitalism was now opposed by the principle of cooperation – collective action which excluded individual competition and the pursuit of profit.[1]

The idea of 'socialism' in this sense appeared practically simultaneously in both Britain and France towards the end of the 1820s and the beginning of the 1830s.[2] While those who propagated socialism and considered it an alternative to the existing social order were in no way unanimous in their views on the details of the structure of this desirable 'just' society, they all at least shared the belief that the preconditions for a humane world freed of exploitation could be created on the basis of communal settlements and production cooperatives. At this point in time certainly, the theorists were limited to more or less vaguely defining the future form of society. No one could go beyond this to offer a theory which could adequately tackle the problems of the transition to a socialist society and in particular confront the contradictory interests of social classes which ensured that proposals for social change were always met with inertia and hostility. This failure is explicable by the lack of any understanding of the laws of motion, the possibilities of development and the class structure of the still incipient capitalism, so that 'immature theories corresponded to the immature level of capitalist production and the immature development of classes'.[3] At this stage the treatment of questions of political economy remained one-sided, unconnected to any analysis of the totality of the structural and developmental determinants of capitalism. The partial analysis frequently led to the belief that if the defects of the system were pointed out, then this by itself would be enough to produce within the ruling class the rational desire to abolish repression and exploitation. Alternatively, the advocates of cooperative forms of production believed that their proposals would attract the support of the rich and powerful, and that once such cooperative institutions were set up, then the internal dynamic of this superior form of production would gradually transform the existing order.

The problem of the private ownership of the means of production moved only slowly into the centre of economic studies, only in Marx's own work becoming for the first time the centre of analysis. Before Marx there had already been a few calls for the socialization of the means of production as a necessary precondition for the resolution of social tensions and for the emancipation of the lower classes, but by contrast other opponents of industrial capitalism claimed instead that the aim of a 'just' society could only be achieved by distributing the means of production equally to all producers or by reforming income distribution on the basis of the demand that all should receive the full yield of their labour.[4]

The full range of positions from which a critique of the social order of capitalism could begin is best presented by examining not just the theorists whose proposals for social reform contained elements of cooperative ideas, but also all those who attempted to overcome the capitalist mode of production, namely the domination of capital over labour. The rationale for this approach lies in the fact that the creation of socialist theory was basically stimulated by the insights of the adherents of cooperative forms of production and of the advocates of a system of small producers, and that its development utilized the arguments of both schools.

That circle of people who have been somewhat superficially subsumed under the label of the 'early socialists' was in fact extremely heterogeneous.

If one attempts to categorize them according to the contents of their theories, then, as has already been hinted, one basic way of differentiating them is according to their attitude to the principle of individual competition: not all those who rejected the capitalist form of production and appropriation also wanted to abolish competition amongst the producers themselves.

That some theorists proposed to retain competition was linked to their commitment to the ideal of a society made up of small producers. In this they were clearly looking backwards into the past, ignoring or only inadequately recognizing the trend of capitalism towards mass factory production, while they also believed that conditions of competition were the only way of providing an incentive for an extension of production.

By contrast, for the theorists who considered the industrial form of production − production linked to machines and factories − as the precondition for satisfying the material needs of society, the obstacle to an optimal development of human abilities was individual competition itself. In their opinion it was here, in the principle of competition, that lay the cause of the contradiction of wealth and poverty: to them it appeared that only cooperation would allow a considerable increase in production and at the same the achievement of their aim of a 'just' distribution of wealth.

Interestingly enough, it was precisely those anti-capitalist theorists who wished to retain competition who were extremely hostile to the state, an institution which according to the dominant beliefs of the time was merely an authority for providing the framework for economic life. Amongst these thinkers, for example Thomas HODGSKIN (1783–1869) and Pierre Joseph PROUDHON (1809–1865), we find the beginnings of an anarchist conception of society, based on the conviction that in the past the state had only represented the interests of the possessing classes and not the interests of society as a whole, and that only the abolition of the state's institutions could restore justice to the individual. In this context belongs the controversy amongst the early agrarian reformers (who will be discussed separately in this study), for their central concern was the interlocking of economic and political power and the alternative possible ways of breaking up concentrations of power.

Apart from the differences which have been mentioned, all the anti-capitalist theorists were united in their rejection of the basic principles of the bourgeois economists, as represented by writers from Malthus and Say to Ricardo and McCulloch. Unlike the latter, for the anti-capitalists there existed no natural law of poverty and no law of population which laid down that every hope of improving the situation of the masses was unrealistic and illusory. The belief that they all shared in a world without poverty stood in direct opposition to the teachings of Malthus. Again and again, the anti-capitalist theorists expressed their conviction that nature had provided adequate means for raising the general level of welfare, and that achieving this was merely a question of a better use of resources and a more equal distribution of the results of labour.

1. The early agrarian reformers[5]

After 1794 in France the counter-revolution began to consolidate itself and partially rolled back the achievements of 1789. In this situation Gracchus BABEUF (1760–1797) developed his plans to establish communism in France by means of a political conspiracy: the extremely egalitarian form of communism which he put forward envisaged the nationalization of all property, the abolition of right of inheritance, the strict regulation of all areas of life, the widest possible simplification and levelling of all needs and also the state distribution of foodstuffs.[6]

As is well known, Babeuf's plans for a *coup d'état* were foiled and he himself sentenced to death. His socio-economic ideas soon passed into oblivion, not least because their impracticability was all too obvious. Babeuf's name remained linked with the idea of a planned political revolution – the introduction of communism by means of conspiracy – a strategy revived again in the 1830s by Louis Auguste BLANQUI (1805–1881).

If Babeuf's economic ideas and objectives were still primitive, at roughly the same period in England two agrarian theorists developed socio-economic models which also aimed at the conquest of inequality, but which from an economic point of view must be considered to be far more mature. The theories of Thomas SPENCE (1750–1814) and Charles HALL (circa 1740–1820) differ widely from Babeuf's plans, and this can be primarily explained by the different level of economic development in the two countries. In England, especially in agriculture, capitalism had already made great advances and consequently awareness of economic problems was far more pronounced than in France. As a result, Spence and Hall were able to put forward proposals for the reform of the agrarian structure which took far more account of the real possibilities of change than Babeuf's plans had done. In fact, the plans of all three had in common only that they all called for the abolition of private ownership in land in order to prevent thereby the emergence of concentrations of economic and political power; in all other respects they diverged.

Even before the French Revolution Spence had become prominent with his plans for socializing the land. In a lecture in 1775 he had demanded the return of the land to the people as a whole in order to create thus the preconditions for a democratization of society.[7] Later he published further writings in which he defined his theories more precisely and attacked ever more sharply aristocratic rule in England.[8]

At the centre of Spence's writings stood the relationship between the state and society. He believed that if the freedom of the individual was to be extended, then the state's independence and decision-making potential had to be restricted as far as possible, since for him the state was an organ of domination and as such inherently tyrannical. On the question of the state Spence thus found himself in opposition to Babeuf, in whose plans the state was allocated wide-ranging powers. In his theories Spence envisaged the transfer of land into communal ownership, the communities being kept small in order to ensure that they were able to govern themselves democratically. To the state as an institution above the communities he wished to allocate only those few tasks which involved the national interest. So that the state and the communities would be able to finance and carry out their collective tasks, land was to be rented by the communities to families and the product passed to the communities and the state in accordance with their financial needs and the tasks allocated to them. Land was not to be farmed collectively, rather each family was to be left to use as it wished the product of the land which it rented.[9]

The theory formulated by Hall in 1805 had a similar aim of agrarian reform but proposed different methods.[10] Already in the works of Adam SMITH (1723–1790) the contradictions of capitalism were incipiently present, and Hall was one of the first to develop these, if in a crude form, into a theory of classes. According to Hall the division of society into rich and poor, for him the characteristic feature of civilization and hence of the capitalist order, originated in the monopoly of power held by the great land-owners. It was their wealth, originally acquired by robbery, which gave them the power to control the labour power of the poor. In order to shatter this power, Hall believed it was not enough just to divide up the large landholdings, as for example the agrarian reformer Thomas PAINE (1737–1809)[11] had already demanded. Unlike Spence, Hall did not consider the possibility of transfering land into municipal ownership, but instead called for the centralized nationalization of land.[12]

The divergent conceptions of the state which Spence and Hall held became clear once again in an exchange of letters between them in 1807[13]. While Spence feared that if the state were granted much authority, then it would become autonomous and tyrannical, and could see no possibility of such a state being effectively controlled by the people, Hall was unable to share these fears. For him there was no reason why it should not be possible to structure society and all its institutions democratically, thus creating a state the decisions of which would reflect the will of the majority and which would be the expression of a rational agreement between the members of the community.

Neither Spence nor Hall foresaw the necessary structural changes of developing capitalism: thus for example they both either completely neglected the industrial sector or demanded that it should be dramatically limited and even abolished. Nonetheless, their writings drew attention to links between social and economic questions which had until then been largely ignored. In their controversy over power and its concentration they touched on the problem of centralized versus decentralized decision-making authority, a problem which was to come up again and again in the subsequent discussion of economic and political theory.

2. The critics of competition

(a) Saint-Simon and His Pupils

Not all the theorists who saw competition as a destructive element in what seemed to them to be a just society developed alternative socialist economic models. This is true, for example, of Henri DE SAINT-SIMON (1760–1825), whose vision of a new industrial society sprang more from liberal than from socialist traditions of thought. Nonetheless, it has to be recognized that in the last years before his death Saint-Simon concerned himself intensively with the possibilities of improving the situation of the lower classes and diverged from his earlier liberal belief that the cause of the power of the possessing groups was their intellectual superiority.

Despite their basically liberal nature, Saint-Simon's ideas are discussed here because on the one hand he wanted to make coordination and planning of the economy as a whole the basis of the new society, and because on the other hand he intended the state to be deliberately used as an instrument to force scientific progress and the advance of social production.[14] These beliefs, which were developed further by Saint-Simon's supporters, have had a not insignificant influence on the development of socialist models of society.

Saint-Simon's theories arose in the period of the transition from feudalism to capitalism. He himself held the most urgent task to be the abolition of the feudal forms of rule which still partially existed in France.[15] He sketched out the general outlines of a future form of society which would be administered by scientists, industrialists[16] (under which he understood farmers, entrepreneurs, bankers, merchants and workers) and artists in harmonious co-operation. In this society class conflict would no longer exist, since by universal assent it would be the most able individuals who would occupy the highest social positions and would direct the talents of all the citizens for the benefit of all. In the coming epoch the class contradiction would no longer exist which had marked the feudal past – the contradiction between the idlers and the parasitic strata on the one hand and the producing classes on the other – for the achievement principle would be recognized by all as the basis of human social life[17]. For Saint-Simon the fact that class conflict between capitalists and workers did still exist in England, where feudal structures belonged to the past, was merely the result of the employers there not having adequately explained to the workers the common interests which both groups shared.[18].

For Saint-Simon the period that was approaching would be one of universal happiness, the community of producers would become reality and cooperation amongst all workers would lead to the full self-realization of every individual. Politics, he held, would then become identical with the direction and planning of production: individual competition amongst the producers would thus belong to the past, while the traditional role of government would either be replaced by the administration of production or subordinated to it.[19]

This new industrial society would be a hierarchically ordered society, with the most important decision-making powers allocated to the most industrious individuals, in particular to the bankers. Saint-Simon held individual property to entail social functions and obligations – he himself did not demand any socialization of the means of production. In order to overcome as quickly as possible the repression and disorder that still existed in society, and above all in order to liberate the proletariat, he proposed that state measures should be introduced to create work, and that these should have as their objective the physical, moral and intellectual improvement of the workers' conditions.[20]

Saint-Simon's pupils[21] were decisively influenced by the developing capitalist system and they reached new insights and understandings which were partially or completely absent from the work of their master. They broke with Saint-Simon's harmonistic view of society, because they believed they recognized that unless further structural reforms were carried out, industrial society would necessarily remain a class society and a society dominated by exploitation.

Much more strongly than Saint-Simon, these thinkers emphasized the disadvantages of individual competition and demanded its abolition by means of the association of producers. In their opinion such an association was the way to remove exploitation and open the door to a system of reward according to achievement. As necessary parallel measures they saw the extension of inheritance tax and the transfer of inheritance rights from the family to the state. They believed a central bank should administer the means of production in their entirety and be responsible for paying everyone according to their ability: bank credit was to be centrally organized in the interests of the workers and it was assumed this would lead to a lowering of the interest rate, so denying the parasitical strata the basis of their existence.[22]

In their theoretical investigations Saint-Simon's pupils reached more radical conclusions than their master. They believed that the conditions under which the workers produced within capitalism were not basically different from the situation of slaves and serfs: the fact that the worker was not in a relationship of personal dependence could not disguise the fact that exploitation and antagonism between the classes continued to exist as before. For them only a fundamental change in the rights of property, with as its core the nationalization of the means of production, could ensure a final end to the exploitation of some human beings by others.

However, after 1830 Saint-Simon's followers began to include mystical and theocratic ideas in their theories; in addition they dissociated themselves from the Lyons workers' rising of 1831. As a result, the Saint-Simonists lost their attraction for the working classes and were soon reduced to an uninfluential sect.

(b) Fourier

While Saint-Simon had tried to sketch out the basic outlines of an industrial society which would overcome national boundaries and which would be unsullied by any class antagonisms, Charles FOURIER (1772–1837) was concerned to deduce the ideal form of community life from the physical structure of human beings. At a time when industrialization was slowly beginning to spread in France and it was becoming unmistakeably clear that capitalism was necessarily accompanied by the alienation of the workers from their product, Fourier wished to reconcile people with their labour. The core of his theories was the notion of human self-realization through labour. For him the main obstacle on the way to a harmonious and just society was not the division of society into capitalists and workers, but lay in people's failure to orientate themselves to their own inner desires.

The 'economy of passions' was thus for Fourier the key problem of the future. If through varied and mutually complementary forms of work it were possible to satisfy the twelve passions which he believed people possessed, then the leap into the new society would succeed. For him it was the protest of unsatisfied passions, and not the revolt of an exploited class, which was the force which would overcome the existing society.[23]

To this end Fourier developed a model of largely agriculturally based collective settlements which he named "*Phalanstères*", and in which, so he assumed, both capitalists and workers could live peaceably together without any interference by the state. The three elements of production – capital, labour and talent – were to be rewarded in the ratio of four-twelfths, five-twelfths, three-twelfths.[24] In order to create the preconditions for this new social order he demanded a drastic restriction of trade (which he described as robbery)[25] and the replacement of individual competition with competition between cooperatives. Fourier described in glowing colours the financial and moral advantages of the *phalanstères* which would for the first time create the possibility of a wide expansion of production and thus falsify Malthus's law of population.[26]

To his death Fourier remained an outsider and always found it impossible to attract any financial support for his plans. Only after his death was his pupil Victor-Prosper CONSIDÉRANT (1809–1893)[27] able to find anyone who was interested in financially supporting the creation of cooperative settlements – incidentally without any great success. Fourier's ideas necessarily failed: his form of producers' cooperatives did not take account of the contradictions between the classes and to a certain extent they have to be seen as a flight from the reality of industrial capitalism. However, in his own time his vehement struggle against trade was in no way anachronistic: between 1807 and 1808 in England there was also a lively discussion of the advantages and disadvantages of both trade and the industrial form of production. Here however the English critics of trade certainly did diverge from Fourier's own intentions, since they basically represented the interests of the English landed aristocracy. Fourier's rejection of central planning methods such as those Saint-Simon had proposed resulted from his belief that the cooperative settlements (to comprise from 1,600 to 1,900 people) would themselves be in a position to determine the extent and form of their production.

Many of Fourier's ideas may well have been naive and unrealistic. Nonetheless, his criticism of bourgeois relationships − *inter alia* his comments on the position of women in society[28] − and his proposals for bringing work and people into harmony must definitely be seen as shrewd and are still of interest today.

(c) Blanc

Louis BLANC (1811−1882) was one of the sharpest critics of the system of individual competition. He held that the cause of the prevailing misery was the competition of all against all. This led, so he argued, to concentration of the economy and to excessively high prices; it not only impoverished the workers but also threatened the existence of a large part of the bourgeoisie itself. In order to liberate society from these evils and above all in order to resist the continual devaluation of human labour, Blanc campaigned for his aim of the 'organization of labour'. However he believed that a future society structured on cooperative principles could not come into existence without the aid of the state. In his plan for a 'governmental' or state socialism the state, once it had been democratically reconstituted, would have the task of operating as the banker of the poor, enabling cooperative workshops to develop under its control. Blanc proposed that the coal mines, railways, banks and insurance system should be nationalized and the profit from them used to finance cooperative production. Alongside this cooperative sector the private economy would continue to exist, but Blanc was absolutely convinced that because of what he believed to be its enormous advantages, the cooperative system would within a short time extend over the whole society and displace all of the capitalist firms.[29]

In France after the revolution of 1848 favourable conditions really seemed to exist for the realization of Blanc's ideas − numerous state subsidized workshops were set up in order to absorb the unemployed. Yet the experiment quickly collapsed, partly because of a lack of organization and partly because of the rapidly increasing influence of conservative forces.

In his ideas for changing society Blanc had misestimated both the alleged advantages of his own plans and also the relations of political power: since they could fix wages with no regard for any ethical or social principles, private firms would inevitably be more profitable and so more competitive than cooperative workshops could ever be; all quite apart from the fact that the bourgeois state could hardly be expected to willingly plan its own demise.

(d) Owen

Robert OWEN (1771−1858) was the most well known of the British social reformers of the 19th century. The fact that he and his proposals for social reform attracted so much attention was not so much the result of any originality of his ideas, but rather because of the attempts that were made to realize them in practice. As a manufacturer Owen owned a large spinning mill in the Scottish village of New Lanark, and it was here after

1800 that he began to apply new methods of organizing the labour process and also of educating children. In 1813 he published *A New View of Society*[30] in which he assessed his previous work and attempted to interest both politicians and scientists in his experiments. For Owen it had long been clear what were the effects on the workers of industrialization with its increasing factory work. In Britain misery had become more and more widespread; particularly in 1811 and 1812, organized groups of machine breakers had systematically destroyed machines on a wide scale, seeing in these the cause of their own misery. For Owen this by itself was enough to make him place the social question at the centre of his concerns.

Owen had reorganized his own factory, reducing the work periods and also setting up a model system of school and pre-school education. He wanted others to emulate these educational and factory innovations and it was with such proposals that he first attempted to gain public attention. The core of his ideas was taken over from William GODWIN (1756–1836), namely the belief that people were basically formed by their environment and that hence they could be shaped as was desired by merely altering their external circumstances.[31]

Owen's ideas at first attracted in particular the attention of politicians, for his proposals seemed to show the possibility of resolving the opposition between wealth and poverty without challenging the political system and without endangering the traditional basis of authority. However, once Owen began to be concerned with more than the narrow area of his own factory, once he started to put forward proposals for abolishing poverty which involved changes in society as a whole, then nearly all of those who had initially listened favourably to his proposals for factory reform now distanced themselves from him. The moment that Owen took the first step towards criticism of basic economic doctrines and branded the principle of competition and the unrestricted pursuit of profit as obstacles to economic progress, then he found himself completely isolated.[32] His fellow human beings' reason and understanding, from which he had expected so much, did not in fact provide him with any followers. Since at the same time he had cultivated anti-democratic and paternalistic ideas, he gained no support either from the side of the workers.

Owen's criticisms of the theories of the classical economists are evidence of his talent for sharp observation of real social and economic relationships. His theory of under-consumption[33] was certainly extremely under-developed, but its stress on the existing discrepancies between production and consumption made it contrast favourably with the equilibrium theories as developed by economists from Say onwards. The post–1815 crisis had convinced him that the depressed economic situation was caused by the masses' lack of purchasing power. In this belief he found himself in agreement with his contemporaries Simonde de SISMONDI (1773–1842) and Fourier.

Owen in no way shared the bourgeois economists' trust that the laissez-faire principle (i.e. the demand that the state should play only a minimal economic role) should be supported because of its alleged guarantee that the economy would tend towards overall equilibrium if only left alone. With his own eyes he saw in Britain the vast army of the unemployed which, according to the claims of the equilibrium theory, should not have existed at all. He also did not believe that unemployment would disappear as soon as (as Malthus demanded) the poor laws were abolished or taxes and customs duties reduced. Owen's own proposals for conquering unemployment were radically different from those of the classical economists. He demanded a state policy for creating work and in 1817 put forward for the first time his plan for so-called 'Villages of Cooperation'.[34] The structure of these cooperative production communities was directed against the existing system of profit and competition; they were intended both to create new jobs and also to produce a considerable expansion of social production as a whole.

Although with his plans and demands Owen found himself almost totally isolated, from then on he made great efforts to criticize the theoretical system of the political economists. In his 'Report to the County of Lanark' Owen was one of the first to attempt systematically to apply the labour theory of value in the interests of the working classes themselves, formulating the basis of the subsequently continually resuscitated principle of the workers' right to the full yield of their labour.[35] He also opposed Malthus's views on the relation between the development of the forces of production and the increase in the material welfare of the population.[36] On the basis of his own experiences in New Lanark he could realistically assess the possibilities of an expansion of production as a result of technical progress; his environmental theory of personality, strengthened by his educational experiences, gave some plausibility to his claim that the birth rate could be lowered through responsible education and improved social relationships.

When Owen realized that in Britain no one was prepared actively to support his plan for communities of producers, he went to America and invested a large part of his property in a cooperative project named 'New Harmony', which however only lasted a short time. In 1829 he returned to England disillusioned, but ready to play a leading role in the newly strong trade union movement. With his help in 1832 an exchange bank was founded based on the labour theory of value, giving out labour money and carrying out transactions on the basis of the value of labour. Yet this project too failed to achieve any long-lasting success.[37]

At first sight the production communities of Owen and Fourier seem to have much in common with each other. Yet despite the parallels the differences are in fact very large. Fourier was basically still locked in the pre-industrial period, and at the same time the capital relationship – i.e. the separation of the wages of labour and the profit of capital – was something he basically did not wish to disturb. Both men's cooperative ideas were initially based on an intensified cultivation of the land, but Owen took industrial production much more into account. Owen also wanted to allow capital only a fixed maximum level of interest, hoping at the same time that the capitalists would take the long-term view and soon would give up their interest once they saw the advantages of the new system.[38] Not least importantly, Owen and Fourier also differed in that Fourier was sceptical of state authority and called for a decentralized structure in order to reduce the possibilities of state intervention, while Owen had a much more positive relationship to state institutions and attempted to win them over as protectors and promoters of his plans.

However, both Owen and Fourier shared with the other social reformers the belief that ultimately the power of reason would overcome all disagreements. For them the class struggle was not the motor of social change but rather a transient expression of the human irrationality entailed by the times in which they lived.

(e) Owen's Followers

Like Saint-Simon and Fourier Owen had a number of followers who took up his ideas and developed them – largely in a somewhat modified form. The most well known of these was clearly William THOMPSON (1783–1833). On the basis of Bentham's principle of the greatest happiness of the largest number Thompson supported Owen's rejection of competition and attempted to work out a synthesis of utilitarianism and cooperatism based on the idea of collective property. Unlike Owen however, Thompson did not hold that an alternative form of economic organization could be created by appealing to the state. Much more than Owen he saw the government as a class-specific institution, the interests of which differed decisively from those of the working classes. He stressed therefore the basic principle of autonomous and independent workers' organizations, wanting also, and again in opposition to Owen, society to be organized on democratic principles and for the workers to share in all decisions.[39]

Thompson, much more than Owen, in developing his theory took into account the interests and level of consciousness of the workers. In that he supported the democratic demands of the lower classes and integrated them into his model, he was able in the 1820s to popularize Owen's plans and gain many adherents. Nonetheless, he shared with Owen the illusion that the ideal of a society based on cooperative institutions could in the end be achieved even against the will of the state. Just like the philanthropist of Lanark, Thompson believed that the victory of the cooperative order over capitalism would be natural and inevitable.

Like Fourier, Thompson drew up a detailed study of the future organization of production cooperatives and was a prominent early champion of the liberation of women.[40]

How the new society was actually to be achieved was an open question which the other adherents of Owen's ideas either ignored, or only answered in a way which took no account of the opposing forces. Thus John GRAY (1799–1850),[41] John F. BRAY (1809–1895)[42] and Minter MORGAN (1782–1854),[43] to mention only the most important, were all agreed that competitive capitalism destroyed humanity and created insurmountable obstacles to human self-realization. They all opposed the basic principles of bourgeois political economy – above all when after Ricardo's death the economists began to be primarily interested in preserving the status quo and a bland apologia replaced the critical potential which Ricardo's own theory clearly had contained. Owen's adherents attacked the existing system of private property, calling for the workers to unite in pursuit of their just interests and demanding that the exchange process should be reorganized according to the labour theory of value.

Nonetheless, however plausible their theories were in detail and however accurate their criticism of the bourgeois economists was, their views of how society was actually to be changed remained, like their ideas of a 'just' social order, vague and utopian. Their principle that the individual workers should be allowed to receive the full value of their labour made clear that they had not recognized capitalism's tendency to concentrate production, and that therefore allocating the produce of labour on an individual basis was now impossible. Equally, they assumed that what they held to be a just economic order could be created by a reform of the monetary system or by intervention in the distributive sector, and they thus ignored the fact that the major obstacle to the realization of their plans was the ruling classes themselves.

3. The individualist anti-capitalist theorists

Strictly speaking the theorists who rejected both capitalism and a system based on the association of producers did not make any direct contribution to socialist economic thought. However, these theorists included some of the most distinguished critics of political economy, and if the critique of both bourgeois society and the economic theories which are accepted by it is seen as a precondition for the formation of socialist ideas, then it seems sensible and necessary to discuss briefly here the ideas of the individualist anti-capitalists.

The liberation of the suppressed and exploited classes was the primary aim of the thought and action of all those who opposed bourgeois society. However, they believed they could reach this objective by differing means and by differing routes. The adherents of cooperative methods of production had made the existing system of competition the key to the possibility or impossibility of social emancipation. To them the liberation of humanity appeared only achievable through the abolition of individual economic competition – common collective action was the only guarantee that the yoke of injustice would be broken and the contradiction of wealth and misery overcome.

It was on this question that the basic difference between the cooperatist and the individualist anti-capitalists came to the surface. Hodgskin and Proudhon also attempted to provide methods for the possible conquest of poverty, and because of the contradictions which they showed to exist between wealth on the one hand and material need on the other, they rejected industrial capitalism just as decisively as Owen or Fourier ever did. However, unlike them, they held competition to be a necessary element of every form of society in which justice and freedom were to be the basis of human community life, suspecting that a system of production which was based on cooperatives would also itself entail new forms of dependency and bondage. Equally, they feared that in such a form of production individual incentive would be lost.[44]

The involvement of the state as the means of forcing the transition from a bourgeois capitalist society to what was propagated as a just future society was something which the individualists opposed even more strongly. In so far as that they made the state and its supporting institutions responsible for social defects, they, like Hodgskin, came close to anarchistic ideas, or, like Proudhon, explicitly demanded anarchy as the realization of a social order free of domination.[45]

Beliefs such as these were not new. Basing himself on the ideas of the Enlightenment, William Godwin had already traced the concentration of economic and political power back to the existence of state institutions and had held their abolition to be the necessary precondition for any form of society free of domination. Like Thomas Paine before him, Godwin's criticism of bourgeois conditions extended to property and its constitutional roots. In Godwin's opinion, the distribution of property provided the key to the problem of 'political justice'. Unlike Paine however, Godwin did not aim at breaking up concentrations of economic power by dividing the land, but instead expressed the conviction that the spread of reason and understanding would itself open the way to an egalitarian and anarchistic society. Once this situation was reached, nobody would have any interest in the acquisition of private riches, while at that same moment every state institution for regulating relationships between people would also become superfluous.[46]

Piercy RAVENSTONE (d. 1830) and Thomas Hodgskin were probably decisively influenced by Godwin's ideas, but they were more interested than Godwin had been in the findings of the bourgeois economists. In particular, they were stimulated by Ricardo's labour theory of value to try to find a different interpretation for it to that on which Ricardo's own work was based – an interpretation which, unlike Ricardo's own, did not provide a justification for the capitalist system. They showed that the labour theory of value led to the inescapable conclusion that both rent and interest were unjustified deductions from the value of the product which was created by the workers alone.[47] From this they deduced the demand that the total product belonged to the workers and must therefore be returned to them. Essentially for both of them it was however only the excesses of capitalism – in particular exploitation and the existence of a parasitical capitalist class – which they wanted to abolish. By contrast, they found quite acceptable and actually wished to retain the real core of capitalism, namely a society of independent individuals who as producers stood in mutual competition with each other.

Like other contemporary critics of the dominant economic theories, Ravenstone and Hodgskin also pointed out that there was a close connection between the growth of population and that of the food supply. Malthus's population theory, which had denied this link, was therefore false and misleading.[48]

Ravenstone, Hodgskin and Proudhon believed that the nearest to an ideal society would be a nation of artisans and small farmers. Hence it is understandable that no part of Owen's plans had any attraction for any of them at all. On the one hand they were sceptical and critical of the form of factory-based production which Owen himself propagated and practised, on the other hand they probably shared the judgement of the petit-bourgeois democratic agitator William COBBETT (1762–1835), who had branded Owen's cooperative manufacturing plants as the workhouses of the future.

Amongst the various fractions of the anti-capitalist theorists there soon arose a sometimes vehement controversy over the advantages and disadvantages of the different forms of organization of labour. Thus in 1827 Thompson opposed the cooperative principle to Hodgskin's ideal of a society of independent producers.[49] Somewhat later on the other hand, Proudhon criticized the socialists' conception of cooperatives and labour organization.[50] Already in 1840 in his book *What is Property* Proudhon had polemicized against unearned capital income and had stressed the advantages which he claimed for a society of independent small producers.[51] Later too he repeatedly argued that both cooperative production and the active use of the state to create what was considered to be a socialist society would endanger, if not actually suppress, the freedom of the individual. In opposition to such proposals, he recommended mutual aid through credit by means of a bank of exchange which would operate without charging any interest payments. Parallel to this he demanded the radical reduction of taxes and customs duties and the abolition of money. In this way Proudhon was assuming that a reform of capitalist society had to begin with massive intervention in the circulation sphere. Intervention of this sort would then directly affect the sphere of production and so alter the basis of the existing order in the direction desired.[52]

Proudhon's theory looked more to the past than to the future. His specific conception of a form of production based on small farmers and artisans shows the close relationship of his ideas to those of Ravenstone and Hodgskin. None of them could imagine that the tendency towards mass production and factory production was unstoppable and that the accompanying parallel growth of the proletariat would make the class struggle the decisive means of social change. Both Hodgskin and Proudhon believed that it was wrong to try to bring about social change through workers' coalitions and trade unions and this, more than anything else, shows how seriously they misunderstood both the real situation and the ways in which it could be changed.

2

KARL MARX'S CRITIQUE OF BOURGEOIS ECONOMICS

1. Scientific method

The work of Karl MARX (1818–1883) is essentially a *critique of political economy*. This is not a systematic development of the social theories of the early socialists, but nor is it a mere continuation of the economic theories of the English classical economists of the school of Smith and Ricardo. What distinguishes Marx from the early socialists is his methodology. Marx starts from the analysis of particular and at first limited sections of society and only then proceeds towards an investigation of bourgeois society as a whole, an investigation which was able to include all areas of human social life. This approach was firstly holistic, in that it aimed to understand society as a whole, and secondly it was dynamic, that is to say, its perspective was both logical and historical.[1] This methodology enabled Marx to gain new insights into the forms of movement and the developmental tendencies of the capitalist mode of production. In this way, he broke decisively with the early socialists' method of investigation, for in their minds there was always a picture of a future society (even though it lacked any concrete link to reality) and they often thought that the leap from the present into the future needed only a basic change in consciousness in society. The early socialists in their analysis therefore stood above classes and hence, inspired only by the feeling that existing conditions were unjust, they could direct their appeals for spiritual renewal to all social classes. By contrast, Marx's approach is class-specific: his appeals for the revolutionizing of the economic base were not directed to society in general, nor to the ruling classes, but only to the proletariat, since this class was the class which most directly experienced the contradictions of capitalism – it was therefore the class which had a material interest in the overthrow of the system. In the words of the well-known passage of the Communist Manifesto:

> The proletarians have nothing to lose but their chains. They have a world to win.[2]

The major difference between Marx and the classical economists, whose contribution to the development of political economy he repeatedly emphasized, was that his own critique had a historical dimension built into it. Marx rejected the allegedly natural laws of bourgeois society and pointed out the transitory character of the capitalist social order.[3] This conception of political economy as an historical science[4] allowed him both to recognize and to explain the forms of production which had existed before capitalism,[5] and also to formulate the conditions which were necessary for the capitalist form of economy to be transformed.[6] If in this way Marx could criticize the weaknesses and the mistakes of the classical economists and their successors the 'vulgar economists', this was not just because of his undoubtedly deep understanding of the laws of movement of the social and economic structure, but also because of the way in which capitalism had developed since their time − by after 1850 capitalism dominated all relevant areas of production. At the beginning of the nineteenth century neither the classical economists nor the anti-capitalist theorists were able to discern the physiognomy of industrial capitalism. The actual development of the new economic order was slow and, as Marx pointed out, contradicted the beliefs of the economists. In the second half of the nineteenth century developmental tendencies became visible which stimulated Marx to make fundamental revisions of the earlier theories. The often *petit bourgeois* beliefs and demands of the early socialists had revealed themselves to be just as far from reality and just as untenable as were the beliefs of the classical economists with their domination by notions of equilibrium and their commitment to social harmony.

Marx's method of investigating social and economic categories and how these interconnect is 'historical materialism'. In the preface to his *Critique of Political Economy* Marx briefly sketched out the basis of this materialist approach to history:

> In the social production of their life, men enter into definite relations that are indispensable and independent of their will, relations of production which correspond to a definite stage of development of their material productive forces. The sum total of these relations of production constitutes the economic structure of society, the real foundation, on which rises a legal and political superstructure and to which correspond definite forms of social consciousness. The mode of production of material life conditions the social, political and intellectual life processes in general. It is not the consciousness of men which determines their being, but, on the contrary, their social being that determines their consciousness .... Just as our opinion of an individual is not based on what he thinks of himself, so can we not judge of such a period of transformation by its own consciousness; on the contrary, this consciousness must be explained rather from the contradictions of material life, from the existing conflict between the social productive forces and the relations of production.[8]

The analysis of the economic structure of society therefore provided for Marx the key to understanding both the existing contradictions and the transcendence of them. If one wanted to understand bourgeois society and how it functioned, one should not therefore begin with the subjective reasons and beliefs which people hold and with which they explain their actions, but start instead by investigating the real − i.e. the economic −

basis of society. Accordingly, Marx came to the conclusion that 'the anatomy of civic society is to be sought in political economy'.[9]

However, this general characterization of the materialist approach to history does not adequately define Marx's analytical method. As he himself indicated[10] and as up to then the economists had actually done, investigation could begin with 'the real and concrete' – for example, with population. Yet this 'concrete' is 'the unity of a multiplicity of determinations' and as such can only be grasped by way of *reproduction*, that is to say, only after an initial abstraction and then investigation of the individual elements. If one proceeds according to this method, then one reaches ever simpler concepts and comes, in Marx's words, 'from the image of the concrete to an ever thinner abstraction'. Only after these elementary categories have been organized in theoretical and historical terms does the whole present itself as a conceptually structured totality of relations and determinations. The population, to continue with the same example, is according to this method of moving from the abstract to the concrete[11] no longer a 'chaotic image of the whole', as in the earlier economists, but is logically constructed out of the various concepts which have been deduced previously, concepts such as classes, wage labour, capital, value, money, price, etc.

While he was working out his methodology, Marx also changed the plan of his work. According to the plan made in 1857 he intended to write six books, one each on capital, landed property, wage labour, the state, foreign trade and the world market. Only in 1866 did Marx decide on the final arrangement of only four books, one each on the production process of capital, the circulation process of capital, the forms of the process as a whole and finally one on the history of the theory of capital. What was most important about this change was that Marx now removed from the first volume of *Capital* the discussion of competition and credit which had originally been planned and concentrated instead on 'capital in general', that is, on capital's most abstract form. The other books from the plan of 1857 were partly incorporated into the three volumes of *Capital* and partly (i.e. the original volumes 4 to 6), now omitted.[12]

2. The commodity, value and surplus value[13]

Marx begins his analysis of the production process with the analysis of the commodity. He does this because, as the elementary form of the wealth of bourgeois society, the commodity is at the same time both the result and the precondition of capitalist society.

From a superficial point of view the commodity is merely something which satisfies human needs. This quality of usefulness makes the commodity into a use value and so into an object of consumption. Use value depends on individuals' judgements of the commodity's usefulness to them; in itself use value says nothing about the way in which the commodity was actually produced.[14] Every commodity however has a double aspect: it has firstly use value and secondly exchange value. Its use value is the precondition for the commodity existing at all and forms the material basis for the commodity's exchange value. Exchange value itself first appears as the quantitative relationships in which use values are exchanged against each other. That this exchange occurs shows that all commodities must have some element in common in terms of which they can be compared. This common basis to which exchange values can be reduced is the fact that all commodities are the result of labour and are exchangeable in proportion to the abstract human labour objectified in them. This is a comparison which abstracts fully from the use value and from the natural qualities of the particular commodity. Abstract human labour means to say that the different types of concrete useful labour are reduced down to 'mere human labour' and that the value of any commodity is measured by the amount of socially necessary labour time needed for its production. Concrete labour, materialized in use value, is separated from abstract labour, materialized in exchange value, and it is here that the double character of the commodity becomes visible.[15]

Marx's next step is to investigate the value relationship of commodities to each other. Within an exchange economy (i.e. an economy within which the commodity form is the general form of the results of labour) the exchange of commodities presupposes that the value of one commodity in relation to another commodity can be expressed in a particular form. Therefore one particular commodity has to be found which can operate as the general equivalent of all other commodities. This special commodity, which exists as a general measure of value separate from all other commodities, is money.[16]

Exchange value expresses the social linkage between commodity producing individuals – through the medium of money a social relationship between people becomes a social relationship between the products of labour, a 'relationship hidden under a reified veil'.[17] Marx calls this reified relationship the fetish character of commodities. The mystical character of the relationship consists in the fact that in the commodity form

> the social character of men's labour appears to them as an objective character stamped upon the product of that labour; because the relation of the producers to the sum total of their own labour is presented to them as a social relation, existing not between themselves, but between the products of their labour.[18]

In a commodity-producing society individuals experience the social character of their activity, like the social form of their products, as something foreign to them.[19] They willingly subordinate themselves to circumstances whose material exterior they are not able to see through; they are unaware that individuality and uniqueness are negated by exchange value; they subordinate themselves to the power incorporated in money[20] without considering that gold and silver are nothing but the 'direct incarnation of all human labour'.[21] According to Marx, this fetishism of money and of commodities will only be overcome when people take into their conscious and planned control the whole form and process of social life.[22]

So far we have been assuming the existence only of a simple exchange economy, i.e. a society in which the producers own their means of production and where capital and labour have not yet been separated. To work out the nature of the capitalist mode of production, Marx now proceeds to investigate the transformation of money into capital so that he can thereby deduce one of the keystones of his theory, namely surplus value.

Within the circulation sphere of an economy two circuits coexist — the first is the conversion of commodities into money and the reconversion of this money into commodities $(C - M - C)$, the second is the conversion of money into commodities and the reconversion of these commodities back into money $(M - C - M)$, whereby in this second circuit money is turned into capital. The first circuit, $C - M - C$, begins with selling and ends with buying: the money for the sake of which the sale has taken place is therefore immediately spent again. Marx gives no further attention to this transaction since obviously it cannot yield any explanation of how money is transformed into capital. The $M - C - M$ circuit is a different matter, for here the purchaser only spends money 'with the sly intention of getting it back again'[23]. This process however is only worthwhile if at the end of the circuit the amount of money is larger than at the beginning:

> The exact form of this process is therefore $M - C - M'$, *where* $M' = M + M$ = the original sum advanced, plus an increment. This increment or excess over the original value I call 'surplus value'. The value originally advanced, therefore, not only remains intact while in circulation, but adds to itself a surplus-value or expands itself. It is this movement that coverts it into capital.[24]

The question immediately arises how this apparently paradoxical movement takes place. Marx demonstrates that surplus value cannot arise in the circulation sphere but is only realized there.[25] It follows therefore that the transformation of money into capital must occur within the production process itself, and according to Marx that therefore there must be a commodity

> whose use value possesses the peculiar property of being a source of value, whose actual consumption, therefore, is itself an embodiment of labour, and, consequently, a creation of value. The possessor of money does find on the market such a special commodity in capacity for labour or labour-power.[26]

For this to happen the workers must offer their labour power as a commodity for a specific length of time, that is to say, the owner of the means of production and of subsistence must find on the market workers who are free to sell their labour power to him.

Like all commodities, labour-power has a value. This value is determined by the amount of labour time needed for its production, which is in this case its reproduction: 'the value of labour-power is the value of the means of subsistence necessary for the maintenance of the labourer'.[27] Paying the price laid down in the wage contract gives the purchaser, in other words the capitalist, the right to the use value of labour-power.[28]

The process whereby labour-power is consumed presents itself as the production of both commodities and of surplus value: through the valorization process of labour power the capitalist obtains a surplus over and above the equivalent of the value of the labour-power he purchased.[29] Marx calls the part of capital which is turned into labour-power 'variable capital',[30] because in the course of the production process its total value changes. Similarly, he calls 'constant capital' that part of capital which is spent on means of production (i.e. on all the materials and instruments of labour), because the value of this part of capital does not grow in the course of the production process, but is merely transferred from the means of production to the new product.[31]

As labour power is consumed, so is surplus value created. Marx relates the amount of this surplus value to the amount of variable capital employed to give the rate of surplus value (or rate of exploitation) − s:v. This ratio shows the proportion of surplus labour to necessary labour or of unpaid to paid labour. The level of exploitation can be raised in two ways − first by lengthening the labour day, secondly by shortening the necessary labour time. Surplus value obtained in this second way Marx calls relative surplus value.[32]

3. The accumulation of capital;

The conversion of money into capital presupposes that a separation has occurred between the owners of the means of production and the owners of labour power. This is the basis of the capitalist production process and once it exists, then the workers continually produce new surplus value and so continually consolidate the power which exploits them, while at the same time reproducing and perpetuating the conditions through which they themselves are exploited.

> Capitalist production, therefore, under its aspect of a continuous connected process, of a process of reproduction, produces not only commodities, not only surplus value, but it also produces and reproduces the capitalist relation: on the one side the capitalist, on the other the wage labourer.[33]

If the newly produced surplus value is to be turned into capital and the process of accumulation to begin, then new labour must be employed, which in its turn once again produces new surplus value. This continually expanding process can only take place smoothly so long as the capitalist does not consume the surplus value, but instead uses it to employ additional workers who bring him in more than they cost. Accumulation of capital is for the capitalist the most basic civic duty, the capitalist is soon made to realize that every expansion of his own private consumption restricts the expansion of accumulation:

> The development of capitalist production makes it constantly necessary to keep increasing the amount of the capital laid out in a given industrial undertaking, and competition makes the immanent laws of capitalist production to be felt by each individual capitalist as external coercive laws. It compels him to keep constantly extending his capital, in order to preserve it, but extend it he cannot, except by means of progressive accumulation.[34]

The continual increase in the productivity of labour more and more becomes the decisive motor of capitalist accumulation.[35] As accumulation proceeds, the number of workers employed rises too, but ever more important is the use of additional and improved means of production. This raises the proportion of constant to variable capital, meaning that the organic composition of capital, as Marx calls this relationship in value terms, increases as accumulation proceeds.[36]

As the proportion of constant capital rises, normally more workers are also employed, and this in turn can lead to increased wages. However, better wages do not alter the nature of the capitalist production process. Accumulation ultimately leads only to an increase in the proletariat, and higher wages for labour means, in fact, only that the length and the weight of the golden chain the wage-worker has already forged for himself, allow of a relaxation in the tension of it'.[37] Too great an increase in the price of labour power has adverse effects on accumulation, since it causes profits to fall. This in turn leads to a reversal of accumulation and hence makes wages fall again.

> The mechanism of the process of capitalist production removes the very obstacles that it temporarily creates. The price of labour falls again to a level corresponding with the needs of the self-expansion of capital, whether the level be below, the same as, or above the one which was normal before the rise of wages took place.[38]

Accumulation goes together with the concentration and the centralization of capital. Already in the transition from craft production to the capitalist factory one precondition is that capital is concentrated in the hands of individual commodity producers. With production on an expanded scale the amount of capital concentrated under the control of each individual capitalist increases: the general level of concentration is dependent on the growth of the wealth of society.

In the process of capital accumulation old capitals continually divide, while simultaneously new ones form:

> Accumulation, therefore, presents itself on the one hand as increasing concentration of the means of production, and of the command over labour; on the other, as repulsion of many individual capitals one from another.[39]

The concentration of capital in the hands of a few goes together with the merging of already formed capitals. This does not involve any absolute growth of social wealth, what matters is that existing capitals give up their independence and merge (e.g. in joint stock companies).[40] This absorption of individual and mostly small capitals is the result of competition.

As the productivity of labour rises and thus commodities are cheapened, so increasingly only the financially strong firms are able to survive. Financially weak firms are either taken over by the large producers or attempt to expand into areas of production in which competition is relatively undeveloped. Sooner or later, however, here too the same process of concentration and centralization begins. The capitals put together by centralization are the mightiest lever of accumulation; centralization of capital supports and complements the continual technical development and so enables the rapid development of the productive forces.

With the increase in the organic composition of capital the substitution of capital for labour releases labour which partly finds new employment in other branches of the economy. The accumulation of capital thus permanently produces a labouring population which is superfluous to the medium term needs of capital for valorization, and which varies in size according to the economic situation. Marx calls this superfluous labouring population the industrial reserve army.[41] The course characteristic of modern industry, viz., a decennial cycle (interrupted by smaller oscillations) of periods of average activity, production at high pressure, crisis and stagnation, depends on the constant formation, the greater or lesser absorption, and the re-formation of the industrial reserve army or surplus population. In their turn, the varying phases of the industrial cycle recruit the surplus population, and become one of the most energetic agents of its reproduction.[42]

In this way, Marx opposes Malthus's theory of population which alleged that since population increases geometrically while the supply of food only increases arithmetically, there must always exist an absolute over-population. By contrast Marx points out that over-population is only relative, and further, that it cannot be deduced from any natural laws but is the result of the cyclical movement of the production process. Relative over-population, according to Marx, therefore forms a necessary condition for the existence of modern industry.[43]

Although social wealth continually increases, this does not benefit all classes in society equally. Instead, the accumulation of capital goes together with the accumulation of misery:

> Within the capitalist system all methods of raising the social productiveness of labour are brought about at the cost of the individual labourer: all means for the development of production transform themselves into means of domination over, and exploitation of, the producers; they mutilate the labourer into a fragment of a man, degrade him to the level of an appendage of a machine, destroy every remnant of charm in his work and turn it into a hated toil – they estrange from him the intellectual potentialities of the labour process in the same proportion as science is incorporated in it as an independent power; they distort the conditions under which he works, subject him during the labour process to a despotism the more hateful in its meanness – they transform his life-time into working-time, and drag his wife and child beneath the wheels of the Juggernaut of capital.[44]

As for the further development of the accumulation process, Marx clearly was convinced that the capitalist form of production carries within it the seeds of its destruction. Capitalist private property is the negation of individual private property based on the individual's own labour. This contradiction between social production and private appropriation cannot be resolved within the capitalist system. The opposition between the accumulation of wealth and the accumulation of poverty pushes towards the overthrow of the system:

> The monopoly of capital becomes a fetter upon the mode of production, which has sprung up and flourished along with and under it. Centralization of the means of production and socialization of labour at last reach a point where they become incompatible with their capitalist integument. This integument is burst assunder. The knell of capitalist private property sounds. The expropriators are expropriated.[45]

4. Value and price

Under conditions of capitalist commodity production the value of commodities corresponds to the amount of labour time objectified in them. The formula for the value product of a commodity (C) is: $C = c + v + s$, where c is the amount of constant capital consumed, v is the variable capital or paid labour consumed, and s the surplus value or unpaid labour.[46] Marx did not intend value analysis to be the basis of a complete theory of prices, instead he believed that the theory of value was a way of uncovering the inner structure of the capitalist mode of production. Marx was very well aware that in the conditions of developed capitalism the law of value cannot ever operate in its pure form – in other words that prices must diverge from values. However, he did not consider it his task to explain how the price of each individual commodity was formed. The theory of value therefore must not be understood as a theory of price formation, but as a theory of the creation of value and the distribution of income in the economy as a whole. Marx's analysis aims to investigate the distribution of total income between the different social classes and in particular to explain what share of the total product goes to the working class and what share is appropriated by the capitalists in the form of surplus value, and also what major changes can occur over time. However, soon after the publication of the first volume of *Capital*, bourgeois economists were claiming that with the theory of value Marx had got himself into insoluble contradictions, since in reality the prices of commodities were not determined by the amount of labour time objectified in them. The third volume of *Capital* was edited by Engels after Marx's death and its appearance was eagerly awaited. In it Marx attempted to reconcile the 'process of movement of capital as a whole' with the law of value, yet despite or even precisely because of this, after its publication the critics still felt that their initial negative reactions had been justified.[47]

The controversy was over Marx's analysis of the relationship between value and price. After the extensive abstract discussion of value and of exchange value in the first volume of *Capital*, in the third volume Marx aimed to begin to explain the capitalist production process as the unity of production process and circulation process, and thus to approach the form in which the production process actually presents itself on the 'surface of society'. In the course of this analysis Marx showed that the exchange of individual commodities cannot in fact occur according to the formula of $C = c + v + m$. Firstly, the relationship between constant and variable capital varies between the different sectors of the economy – the organic composition of capital is different in the different sectors. Some branches are labour intensive and others are capital intensive, in other words, in some branches variable capital makes up a larger proportion of the total capital employed than it does in other branches. Secondly, price is formed in a different way to value. The value product results from the addition of c, v and s, and here Marx makes the initial assumption that s is the same proportion of v in all branches of production. Prices however are formed on the basis of the cost price $(c + v)$ together with a rate of profit $(p' = m/(c + v))$ which is equalized by competition across all sectors of the economy.[48] If the organic composition of capital varies, then the rate of exploitation and the rate of profit must therefore diverge from each other.[49]

Given these assumptions it is easy to deduce that in most cases value and price must be different. If the prices of commodities and the values of commodities were formed in the same way, then given a varying organic composition of capital in the different branches, the profit rates would have to be different as well, and this would obviously contradict the tendency within capitalism for profit rates to be the same. It follows therefore that in all branches of production where the organic composition of capital differs from the overall average, then prices must lie above or below the corresponding values.[50] Marx clearly recognized and frequently stressed this divergence of prices and values.

Once again we have to remember that the law of value is not concerned with the micro-level analysis of the formation of market prices: value analysis is meant to be a way of locating the laws of movement of capitalism. It should therefore be clear that the theory has to be applied at the level of the economy as a whole. Here it can be shown that the mass of profit is equal to the mass of surplus value, therefore that the variations of prices from values cancel each other out.[51] However, the upper limit of the mass of profit is given by the mass of surplus value, so clearly we are able to say that prices are determined by the law of value. If prices and values can thus be shown to be linked, this strengthens the claim that the analysis of value and surplus values does enable us to understand the process whereby value is created and the value product divided between the working class and the capitalist class.

5. The tendency of the rate of profit to fall

The accumulation of capital is accompanied by an increasing mechanization of the production process, which is the same as saying that the productivity of labour rises: the same amount of labour now is able to work more material and to produce an increased output. In the course of accumulation the mass of material employed in production increases faster than the mass of labour which is employed. From this we can easily deduce that there is a rise in the technical composition of capital, defined as the ratio of the mass of materials to the mass of labour. If, following Marx, we define the organic composition of capital as this relationship expressed in value terms, 'in so far as it is determined by its technical composition and mirrors the changes of the latter'[52] then we can conclude that the accumulation of capital goes together with an increased organic composition of capital. If we further assume that the rate of surplus value remains constant, then it can be shown that the rate of profit $(s/(c + v))$ falls or tends to fall as accumulation continues.[53] This gradual fall in the profit rate in no way rules out

> that the absolute mass of exploited labour set in motion by the social capital, and consequently the absolute mass of the surplus labour it appropriates, may grow; nor, that the capitals controlled by individual capitalists may dispose of a growing mass of labour and, hence, of surplus labour, the latter even though the number of labourers they employ does not increase.[54]

Consequently the fall in the rate of profit results from the decline in the proportion of variable capital in relation to constant capital. With this law Marx wanted to show that the fall in the rate of profit does not result, as Adam Smith had assumed it did, from the increasing competition between capitals nor does it follow, as Ricardo had attempted to prove, from the combination of Malthus's law of population with a declining yield from agriculture. Instead, for Marx, the fall in the rate of profit has to be deduced from the main laws of movement of capital itself.

Marx was not content with this general formulation of the law since he spoke only of a *tendency* of the rate to fall, he also investigated the countervailing tendencies. He himself problematized the assumption that the rate of surplus value is constant and himself explicitly discussed the situation in which the rate of exploitation of labour rises. As a result of this he came to the conclusion that the increase in the rate of surplus value was one factor which determined the mass of surplus value, and hence the rate of profit. The rise in the rate of surplus value

> does not abolish the general law. But it causes that law to act rather as a tendency, i.e., as a law whose absolute action is checked, retarded, and weakened, by counteracting circumstances.[55]

Marx saw another important countervailing tendency in the 'cheapening of the elements of constant capital'.[56] By this he means that the value of constant capital does not increase to the same extent as its physical mass does, and that this has the effect of slowing down the increase in the organic composition of capital. The importance of this devaluation of capital must not be underestimated, especially with rapid and continual changes in technology.[57] Other countervailing tendencies are the 'forcing down of the labour wage below its value' and the growth of the relative over-population, which both express themselves in slower technical progress and reduced substitution of capital for labour. Marx also mentioned as a further countervailing tendency foreign trade, where lack of competition allows commodities to be sold above their value and hence to yield greater profits, thus counteracting the effects of the general law.[58] Marx however believed that these factors could not invalidate the law, for in the long term they have no compensating effects: without these countervailing tendencies:

> it would not be the fall of the general rate of profit, but rather its relative slowness, that would be incomprehensible. Thus, the law acts only as a tendency. And it is only under certain circumstances and only after long periods that its effects become strikingly pronounced.[59]

In the economic literature Marx's law of the tendency of the rate of profit to fall has received considerable attention, but it also led to serious controversy. A recent study by Gilman[60] attempted to test the law empirically and found no clear long-term trend towards a falling rate of profit. However, any such study comes up against the difficulty that it has to transform magnitudes of value (within which Marx's own argument is expressed) into magnitudes of price, while prices themselves have to be taken from official statistics which are usable only with major reservations.

However, Marx's thesis of capitalist stagnation remains important, even though the law of the tendency of the rate of profit to fall cannot be empirically verified and even though his model is based on unconvincing assumptions (it cannot be theoretically demonstrated that the long-term countervailing tendencies must inevitably prevent a fall in the rate of profit.)[61] The importance of Marx's argument is that it shows that if the rate of profit is not to be negatively affected, then capital accumulation has to be accompanied by adequate technological progress. Certainly, the increased mass of constant capital goes together with a devaluation of constant capital, and this limits the rise in the organic composition. However, technical progress, the motor and the corrective of capital accumulation, at the same time involves costs and external effects, and from a long-term perspective it is clear that in the end these can be so great that they have a negative effect on the profit rate.

6. The problem of crisis

For Marx the accumulation of capital always entailed capitalist crisis. Although his work contains no developed theory of crisis, he continually refers to the crisis-ridden nature of capitalist development. Thus in the third volume of *Capital* he writes:

> Crises are always but momentary and forcible solutions of the existing contradictions. They are violent eruptions which for a time restore the disturbed equilibrium. The contradiction, to put it in a very general way,

consists in that the capitalist mode of production involves a tendency towards absolute development of the productive forces, regardless of the value and surplus value it contains, and regardless of the social conditions under which capitalist production takes place; while, on the other hand, its aim is to preserve the value of the existing capital and promote its self-expansion to the highest limit.[62]

Here Marx was opposing in particular those classical economists, such as Ricardo and Say, who had claimed that crises were impossible, merely because every supply automatically created its own demand: for them, accumulation was therefore an automatic and problem free process.[63] While theories of crisis certainly did exist in Ricardo's own time, Ricardo's own equilibrium theory of development left no room for any discussion of crisis at all.[64] In this situation theorists like Lauderdale and Malthus were not alone in seeing the cause of crisis in a lack of demand. In accordance with their conservative political position, such theorists supported the existence of a class of unproductive consumers (amongst whom the aristocracy always figured prominently) as a way of increasing demand. At the same time petty bourgeois theorists such as Sismondi also put forward an under-consumptionist explanation of crisis, and Robert Owen too suspected that capitalism's crisis-ridden development was caused by the low purchasing power of the masses.

Marx however cannot be classified with these early under-consumptionist views. Certainly at one stage he wrote:

> The ultimate reason for all real crisis always remains the poverty and restricted consumption of the masses as opposed to the drive of capitalist production to develop the productive forces as though only the absolute consuming power of society constituted their limit.[65]

However, elsewhere Marx problematized the idea that economic crisis could be explained by the masses' low purchasing power:

> It is sheer tautology to say that crises are caused by the scarcity of effective consumption, or of effective consumers. The capitalist system does not know any other modes of consumption than effective ones, except that of *sub forma pauperis* or of the swindler .... But if one were to attempt to give this tautology the semblance of a profounder justification by saying that the working class receives too small a portion of its own product and the evil would be remedied as soon as it received a larger share of it and its wages increase in consequence, one could only remark that crises are always prepared by precisely a period in which wages rise generally and the working class usually gets a larger share of that part of the annual product which is intended for consumption. From the point of view of these advocates of sound and 'simple' (!) common sense, such a period should rather remove the crisis. It appears, then, that capitalist production comprises conditions independent of good or bad will, which permit the working class to enjoy a relative prosperity only momentarily, and at that always only as the harbinger of a coming crisis.[66]

It was on this basis that Marx opposed calls for the distribution of land to the propertyless peasantry in order to alter the distribution of income and raise the purchasing power of the class of agricultural labourers – a demand which Sismondi had deduced from his own underconsumptionist theory of crisis. Similarly he opposed Owen, who hoped that the same result of increased demand could be achieved by means of his producers' cooperatives.

Clearly therefore Marx did not in fact commit himself to any of the traditional crisis theories. He was himself very well aware that crises are complicated phenomena with a structure and a form which always has to be investigated and analysed in the context of the real development of capitalism. On this point he wrote that 'the real crisis can only be deduced from the real movement of capitalist production, competition and credit'[67] but he never achieved a more detailed formulation of what this involved. Nonetheless, Marx's work does allow us to reconstruct the outline of a theory of crisis along the following lines.

The capitalist system is characterized by the following contradiction: the aim of capitalist production is not to satisfy social needs but to create and increase surplus value – capitalist production is therefore not production for consumption. By itself this reveals the limit of accumulation:

> The *real barrier* of capitalist production is *capital itself*. It is that capital and its self-expansion appear as the starting and the closing point, the motive and the purpose of production; that production is only production for *capital* and not vice versa, the means of production are not mere means for a constant expansion of the living process of the *society* of producers.[68]

As a result of this 'desire of the capitalists ... to enlarge their capital'[69] an overproduction of capital occurs and hence simultaneously an overaccumulation of capital, since production is being carried out without any regard for the market. This overaccumulation finds its manifestation in the tendency of the rate of profit to fall. Basically therefore it can be said that the fall of the profit rate triggers off the crisis and so accumulation comes to a standstill 'at a point fixed by the production and realization of profit, and not by the satisfaction of requirements.'[70]

This argument suggests two different forms in which the crisis-ridden development of capitalism can proceed. In the first form the immediate origin of the crisis is a fall in the rate of surplus value, which leads directly to difficulties in accumulation, in the second form the crisis originates in market problems, i.e. in 'realization problems'. In the first case the labour market can be exhausted in the course of accumulation and so the industrial reserve army disappears. This leads to an increase in the level of wages and hence to a proportionate fall in the rate of surplus value. A falling profit rate as a result of rising wages must sooner or later restrict accumulation – investments are cut back and in turn this can lead to a situation of crisis, since it causes a reduction of variable capital and a fall in wages and effective demand. The conditions for a renewed increase in the rate of accumulation are then recreated in the crisis situation itself.[71] The basic characteristic of the second possible form of development is that the markets for commodities become glutted in the course of accumulation: commodities cannot be absorbed at their value because of the narrow limits on any expansion of the masses' ability to consume. Sales, and with them the realization of surplus value, falter; price competition becomes the only way commodities can be sold. However, since a fall in prices involves also a fall in the profit rate, accumulation is once again negatively affected and the process continues as in the first form of crisis.[72] Whatever concrete form it takes, the crisis always reveals the immanent contradictions of capitalism. In a natural economy crises are only conceivable as natural catastrophes, but in an exchange economy, where money operates as the medium of exchange and where buying and selling are separated from one another, then crisis is inherent in the system itself.[73] In the crisis the two phases of the exchange process – buying and selling – are brought together again:

> It is precisely the *crisis* in which they assert their unity, the unity of the different aspects. The independence which these two linked and complimentary phases assume in relation to each other is forcibly destroyed. Thus the crisis manifests the unity of the two phases that have become independent of each other. There would be no crisis without this inner unity of factors that are apparently indifferent to each other.[74]

Crisis, remarks Marx at another point, is 'precisely the phase of disturbance and interruption of the process of reproduction.'[75] However, contrary to what was often claimed later, this cannot mean that the reproduction process itself[76] can essentially occur smoothly and in equilibrium, nor does it mean that disturbances in the reproduction process can therefore be resolved under capitalist conditions through the introduction of a limited amount of capitalist planning.[77] Marx had never denied that partial crises can be traced back to disproportionalities, but for him such crises were only a form in which the contradictory movement of the whole production process manifested itself. The crisis-ridden nature of capitalist accumulation cannot be explained through a one-sided stress on disparities between individual economic sectors nor through a narrow focus on the limited consumption of the masses. Instead, a theory of crisis has to be based on a differentiated analysis of the laws of movement of capitalism as a whole. Such an analysis has to start from the recognition that, firstly, the basis of capitalism is the valorization of capital without any regard for the limits of the market, and that, secondly, the general conditions of crisis have to be deduced from the general conditions of capitalist production itself.

3

THEORIES OF CAPITALISM UP TO THE OCTOBER REVOLUTION

1. Lassalle and the controversy over the state

Ferdinand LASSALLE (1825–1864) encountered economic theory through Marx. While his controversy with Schulze-Delitzsch showed that his economic studies had not been fruitless,[1] his overall position was not essentially based on economic concerns. Thus his 'Working Man's Programme' (1862/63) derived not from political economy, but from an idealist philosophy of history and of the state, expressed in his belief in the 'unique connection between today's historical epoch and the idea of the working class'.[2]

While for Marx the state was the instrument of the ruling class, for Lassalle the state was the general form taken by the social nature of human individuals. The demand of the 'working class' was not therefore that the existing state should be abolished, but rather that its content should be reformed. For Lassalle universal suffrage was the effective instrument to bring about this change:

> Accordingly the object of the State is to bring man to positive expansion and progressive development, in other words, to bring the destiny of man − that is the culture of which the human race is *capable* − into *actual existence*; it is the *training and development* of the human race to freedom.[3]

This theory of the state provides the background for Lassalle's proposals for improving the conditions of the workers which he put forward a year later in his 'Open Letter of 1863'.[4] Here Lassalle characterized the workers' situation with his dramatic 'Iron Law of Wages';

> Under today's conditions, under the domination of the supply and demand for labour, the wages for labour are determined by this one single iron economic law: the average wage of labour will always be fixed at the standard of living normally necessary in a people to ensure its propagation and the continuation of its existence.[5]

Lassalle accepts here the well known wages theory of classical political economy − wages cannot permanently be either above or below the minimum level of existence. If the workers' conditions improve, then more workers marry, the working population increases and there occurs an over-supply of labour; if wages fall below the existence minimum, then the attendant misery reduces the supply of labour and forces wages upwards once again. Just like Marx, Lassalle realized that the existence minimum is in no way a psychologically 'iron' and permanent fact, but rather it is a condition which is socially determined and hence flexible to that extent. However, whether following Marx or independently of him, Lassalle rightly argued that the workers' standard of living has to be compared not to what it was in previous generations but to what is possible in the present day. Hence any improvement in the workers' situation compared to that of earlier generations, even if it has occured, would not be an argument against Lassalle's wages theory.

Lassalle's alternative to the iron law of wages was the 'right to the full yield of labour'. This he believed was to be achieved by the working class becoming its own employer and so ending the division between the worker's wage and the employer's profit. This abolition of the employer's profit could occur in 'the most peaceful, legal and simple manner'[6] – the workers needed only to organize themselves as their own employers in voluntary producers' cooperatives. The necessary means to get the cooperative movement under way were to be provided by the state, once universal suffrage had transformed it into 'the great association of the working classes'.[7]

Lassalle took over the idea of the producers' cooperative from Louis Blanc. Like Blanc he too prefers to describe the delights of the future society instead of making any concrete analysis of the present, and this brings him methodologically very close to the utopian socialists, without however having their historical justification that the undeveloped level of the forces of production prevented any developed theory. At any rate, even though Lassalle's economic ideas fell far behind what had been already produced by Marx and Engels, his views were to have considerable influence on the German workers' movement. For example, it was Lassalleanism, not Marxism, which dominated the Gotha Programme of 1875[8] and, since it corresponded to the reformist ideas of the period of the Second International, Lassalleanism remained influential even after the official turn to Marxism enshrined in the Eisenach Programme of 1891.

2. The German revisionism debate

By the time the Second International was formed in 1889 Marxism had already become the dominant theory of the international workers' movement. One indication of this was the fact that at its Erfurt party congress in 1891 the German Social Democratic Party (SPD) adopted a Marxist programme, which by and large gained the approval of Engels himself:

> The present draft differs very favourably from the former programme. The strong survivals of outmoded traditions – both the specific Lassallean and vulgar socialistic – have in the main been removed, and as regards its

theoretical aspect the draft is, on the whole, based on present day science and can be discussed on this basis.[9]

One reflection of the official turn to Marxism was a rapidly growing literature for the propagation of Marxist economic theory and for its application to particular issues. In this context should be mentioned the exhaustive study by Karl KAUTSKY (1854–1932) of the agrarian question, an important contribution to the inclusion of the agrarian sector within socialist theory,[11] while the 'revisionism debate' from the end of the 1890s raised basic questions of political economy.

As the 'theoretical arm' of reformism,[12] revisionism was a broad European movement.[13] Within it German revisionism, founded by Eduard BERNSTEIN (1850–1932), held a central position, as is shown by the frequent contemporary identification of revisionism with 'Bernsteinism'. The debate over revisionism in Germany was important internationally not just because of the leading role of the German social democratic party within the Second International but also because Bernstein himself took up a multitude of already existing theoretical ideas before he in his turn as 'the' representative of revisionism influenced other currents of revisionism.

Bernstein took up reformism in the 1890s, but it was only after Engels's death in 1895 that he put forward his own views in public with the spectacular attempt to legitimate reformist politics with a revision of Marxist teachings.[14] Bernstein attacked Marxist theory on three fronts: the materialist view of history, the theory of value and surplus value, and finally what he termed the 'collapse theory' of capitalism[15] — the long-run trends which Marxism assumed existed in the capitalist mode of production towards the polarization of classes, the concentration and centralization of production and an inherently crisis-ridden development of capitalism as a whole.

On the first two points Bernstein's argument is difficult to follow since basically he is arguing not so much against Marx as against a particular interpretation of Marx in which to a certain extent the criticism is pre-ordained. Bernstein reduced the materialist theory of history to a mere economic determinism, understood in a completely mechanistic fashion, and such a view of history is correspondingly easy enough to criticize; equally, under the Marxist theory of value and surplus value Bernstein understood roughly what Marx himself had criticized in his critique of the Gotha Programme as regrettable Lassallean mistakes. To a certain extent these misunderstandings were perhaps caused by the fashion in which Kautsky had popularized Marx's theory, and as a result Bernstein's reasons for his objections to Marxism are less interesting than the conclusion which he arrived at. He argued that Marx's theory of value and surplus value and his political economy in general do not reveal the concrete laws of movement of capitalist development. Instead, Marx's theoretical system is merely a conceptual construction only useful, like others such as the theory of marginal utility, within certain limits. The selection of a particular relevant conceptual construction and the empirical verification of it are tasks which are purely a matter of rationality, reason being understood as something standing outside society and being above any social interests.

On this basis Bernstein proceeded to carry out an empirical test of Marx's theory as he understood it. The result was a total revision of certain central assumptions of Marxist political economy. Appealing to statistics which showed the continuing existence of a large number of small firms, Bernstein challenged the tendency towards the concentration of industry into large firms; in so far as any concentration was occuring, he claimed that this was neutralized by the dispersal of shareholding which meant an effective decentralization of capital (what he termed 'the increasing troops of shareholders – we can call them today armies of shareholders'[16]). Finally Bernstein challenged the claim that capitalism is inherently crisis ridden – a challenge which he expressed rather circumspectly in his rhetorical questions:

> whether the enormous extension of the world market, in conjunction with the extraordinary shortening of time necessary for the transmission of news and for the transport trade, has so increased the possibilities of adjustment of disturbances of trade; whether also the enormously increased wealth of the European states, in conjunction with the elasticity of industrial cartels, has so limited the effects of local or individual disturbances that, at least for the present time, general commercial crises similar to the earlier ones are to be regarded as improbable.[17]

For Bernstein, such criticism of the collapse theory was a necessary preliminary for equally reformist practical political demands.

In Schumpeter's words, Bernstein was 'an admirable man but ... no profound thinker and especially no theorist'.[18] The theoretical weaknesses of his position were immediately pointed out by Rosa Luxemburg[19] and Karl Kautsky[20] in their comments on his arguments. As for the real core of Bernstein's theoretical revisions of Marxism, his empirical predictions, these now appear as classic examples of the consequences of theoretical confusion. For example, Bernstein opposed the concentration thesis by pointing out the continued economic viability of ... farriers' and wheelwrights' workshops.[21]

Any Marxist discussion of Bernstein has to take as its central point the methodology of revisionism. Bernstein can be treated as an exemplary case of revisionism as a form of theory, that is of a form of theory which starts from Marx's work, which subjectively understands itself as Marxist, but which nonetheless objectively operates by analysing Marxist theory from the standpoint of bourgeois science and thus amounts to no more than a methodological dissolution of Marxism. Bernstein had no comprehension of the special character of Marx's *critique* of political economy as the abolition and transcendence of bourgeois science; indeed, reminiscing twenty-five years after his sensational break with Marxism, he could claim that in a way Marx himself had been the first revisionist:

It is no accusation against Marx, but on the contrary a recognition of the scientific character of his work, if we point out the fact that the further his analysis of the functioning of capital advances, the closer it comes to what the bourgeois economists have since discovered.[22]

In this way Bernstein could praise someone like F.A. Lange[23] for what he termed the latter's combination of 'sincere and fearless commitment to the liberation of the working class' with 'high scientific objectivity'. However, the paradox is that within Bernstein's understanding of science 'scientific objectivity' is irrelevant for socialist commitment, for this can only rest upon a purely emotional partisanship. Quite apart from whether one considers it politically correct or not, such a position was exactly what Marx and Engels wanted to overcome through their own critique of political economy. Further, the widespread acceptance of Bernstein's revision of Marx was not the result of its being theoretically consistent or yielding reliable predictions. Bernstein's popularity instead showed that despite official recognition of Marxism within the working-class movement, there was still a widespread latent resistence to a socialist theory which entailed uncomfortable political consequences.

3. The Russian revisionism debate

'Bernsteinism' counted as the most important tendency within revisionism and given its wide influence this was quite justified. However, from the point of view of the history of theory the Russian revisionism debate is actually more important. The Russian debate in general remained at a higher theoretical level, even the arguments which were ultimately defeated remained important for the development of socialist economics, and the criticisms led to insights into the nature of the accumulation process which are still relevant for contemporary discussion.

The Russian revisionism debate originated in the controversy in the 1890s between the populists, or 'Narodniks', and the legal and the revolutionary Marxists over the chances of capitalist development in Russia.[24] The Narodniks held that the possibilities of capitalist development in Russia were extremely restricted: on the internal market the poverty and the low purchasing power of the peasant masses made any expanding valorization of capital impossible, while on the external market expansion was balked by competition from the more advanced economies. Both the legal Marxists (Struve, Bulgakow, Tugan-Baranowsky) and Lenin as the representative of revolutionary Marxism opposed this position on the basis of partly similar arguments, if for divergent political reasons. Lenin was later to characterize this alliance as 'the combination of manifestly heterogeneous elements under a common flag to fight the common enemy (the obsolete social and political world outlook).'[25]

The legal Marxists wished to demonstrate that capitalism could develop in Russia and they backed up their arguments by appealing to the Marxist theory of capitalist development. The arguments of Struve and Bulgakow initially focused on the Russian situation and were subsequently generalized by Michael TUGAN-BARANOWSKY(1865–1919), whose works were also published outside Russia and influenced the subsequent theoretical discussion within German social democracy.[26] Tugan-Baranowsky considered that the real core of the Marxist theory of capitalist development is to be found in the schemata of expanded reproduction in the second volume of *Capital*.[27]

In this interpretation Tugan-Baranowsky gave a typically 'neo-equilibrium' slant to the reproduction schemata: Marx's proof of the *possibility* of expanded reproduction now became in Tugan-Baranowsky's hands an objective tendency of the capitalist economy towards regular and harmonious growth:

> These schemata must be taken as evidence for what is in itself a very simple thesis, even though it is one which easily leads to objections if the reproduction process of capital is not adequately understood. Capitalist production creates its own market. If it is possible for social production to be expanded, and if there are sufficient forces of production for this, then given a proportional distribution of social production, demand must expand to correspond to the increased production.[28]

In the reproduction schemata Marx assumes for purposes of illustration a continuous accumulation of capital. Tugan-Baranowsky takes this purely illustrative assumption to reflect the basic tendency of capitalist accumulation, never posing the question of whether and under what conditions this accumulation will actually be undertaken by the capitalists. Consequently enough, for Tugan-Baranowsky crises in capitalism are merely the result of disproportionalities between the different branches of the economy:

> Every non-proportional distribution of social capital necessarily leads to the overproduction of certain commodities. However, since the sectors of production are closely interconnected with each other, a partial overproduction of some commodities can easily become a general overproduction of commodities – the commodity market is flooded with unsold commodities and prices collapse.[29]

Certainly, if those who organize production were able to ascertain exactly the level of demand for the commodities they produce, and if they could also freely move factors of production between the different branches of industry, then stable development would be possible. Within capitalism however this is prevented by the system's most basic characteristic – the unplanned nature of social production itself.

Despite his Marxist vocabulary then, Tugan-Baranowsky had an extremely one-sided understanding of Marx. While he claimed that he 'by and large belonged to the Marxist school',[30] this has to be set against the fact that he decisively rejected key elements of Marxist theory – the theory of value and surplus value, the deduction of crises from the movement of the profit rate, and generally the laws of movement of capitalism which Marx works out in the third volume of *Capital*. Tugan-Baranowsky was influenced by Marx, but he was certainly not a Marxist in the sense of Marxism as the 'critique of political economy': Marxism's influence on him went together with that of marginal utility theory and utopian socialism. Indeed, from early on Tugan-Baranowsky hoped to produce a synthesis of these three different tendencies;[31] his own statements on the political advantages of one or the other theory are contradictory and very soon he no longer even considered himself a Marxist.[32]

While Tugan-Baranowsky argued that capitalism could develop in Russia despite the apparently limited possibilities, the Narodniks used these limitations to challenge the historical role of the Russian working class and to argue for their own aim of a uniquely Russian form of peasant socialism. Hence for LENIN (1870–1924) the vital question was to use the proof that capitalism could develop in Russia to show the validity in Russia, just as elsewhere, of a Marxist class analysis and hence of the leading political role of the proletariat.[33]

Like the legal Marxists, Lenin too appealed to Marx's analysis of expanded reproduction as proof that the internal market could grow at the same pace as the economy's production potential. Indeed, while Marx for his model assumes a constant relation between income and production in order to simplify his examples, Lenin argues that a relative lag of consumer purchasing power is actually no obstacle to capitalist growth, since it is compensated for by the rising organic composition of capital and the over-proportional growth of the production of production goods. This tendency for the growth in consumption to be slower than the growth in overall production can even be considered as a law: since according to the general law of capitalist production constant capital grows faster than variable capital, the department of total social production which produces the means of production must in fact grow faster than the department which produces the means of consumption.[34]

Lenin's criticism of the legal Marxists begins at the point where they, in the words of Rosa Luxemburg, proved more than had to be proved – where they moved from showing the general possibility of capitalist development (and in particular, the possibility of capitalist development in Russia), to attempting to prove that capitalism could last for ever.[35]

Lenin demonstrated that the neo-equilibrium position of the legal Marxists was based on an incomplete and so inadequate understanding of Marxist theory. The legal Marxists accepted certain results of Marx's work while ignoring the law of movement of capitalist development and in particular ignoring its antagonistic character. Already in Struve's work Lenin found that the arguments were rooted in 'an objectivism that describes the process in general, and not each of the antagonistic classes whose conflict makes up the process.'[36]

Tugan-Baranowsky argues equally one-sidedly, examining the schemata of expanded reproduction apart from the real laws of movement of capitalism. Against Tugan-Baranowsky's theory of proportionality Lenin held that disproportionality in the Marxist sense is not a question of how skilfully the various sectors of the economy are coordinated, but is rather the inevitable result of capitalism's inherent discrepancy between the ability to produce and the ability to consume. Like the other real contradictions of capitalism, this certainly does not prevent capitalism from developing, but at the same time it does explain capitalism's historically transient nature.[37] If one remembers the political reasons for the legal Marxists' arguments, people who were in Lenin's later words, 'very moderate folk' and basically 'bourgeois democrats'[38] then their one-sided interpretation of Marx is hardly surprising.

Such criticisms however have not in the long run prevented socialist theoretical discussion from in fact accepting the validity of the legal Marxists' starting point, namely the deduction from the reproduction schemata of a theory of stable capitalist development and accumulation. And this has happened despite Lenin's own prescient warning:

> Schemata alone cannot prove anything: they can only *illustrate* a process, *if its separate elements have been theoretically explained*.[39]

4. Rudolf Hilferding: the concentration and centralization of capital

The rest of this chapter is concerned with the work of Rudolf Hilferding, Rosa Luxemburg, Nikolai Bukharin, V.I. Lenin: theorists who at the beginning of the twentieth century developed Marxist political economy to take account of the socio-economic changes that had occured after Marx's own time. Despite their divergent methods and different conclusions, all four of them share a common central problem: the relationship between the continuing accumulation, concentration and centralization of capital in the metropoles on the one hand, and the imperialist expansion of capital on the other.

In 1910, after he had already become well known for his remarkable reply to Böhm-Bawerk's criticisms of Marx,[40] Rudolf Hilferding published his *Finance Capital*. In his own words, this was an attempt 'to grasp scientifically the economic phenomena of recent capitalist development.'[41] Concretely, these new phenomena were 'those processes of concentration manifested in "the abolition of free competition" through the formation of cartels and trusts together with the ever closer relationship between bank capital and industrial capital.'[42]

It is useful, if somewhat arbitrary, to distinguish between the short and the long term aspects of Hilferding's study – between his analysis of the contemporary situation and his predictions for the future of capitalism. Hilferding's theory has largely become known through this second, predictive aspect, and in fact this has not always been to its advantage.

Capitalist development, according to Hilferding, is characterized by three long-term trends:

1 As accumulation continues industry becomes more and more dependent on the banks, since they are the source of the finance it needs, while because of the rising organic composition of capital and hence the lengthening of the turnover period of capital, this finance becomes increasingly long-term finance. As a result an ever larger part of capital in industry does not belong to the industrialists who actually use it. Capital becomes 'finance capital': in Hilferding's definition, 'capital at the disposal of the banks and utilized by the industrialists'.[43]

2 The centralization of capital which can be seen in industry continues irresistibly for two reasons. Firstly, the cartels and trusts use their power in the market to gain extra profits and thus force their non-cartellized partners towards an equal degree of concentration and centralization as the cost of their own survival. Secondly, the finance capital invested in industry has an interest in reducing competition, both between the different firms within one particular branch of industry and between the different branches themselves. The same multifarious relationships which lead to finance capital wishing to reduce competition also enable it to achieve this aim. The centralization process therefore knows no economic limit:

> The end result of the process would be a general cartel, in which the whole of capitalist production would be regulated consciously by one authority able to determine directly the level of all production in all areas.[44]

3 The same law of centralization applies equally to the banks themselves, so that in the end:

> One bank or one banking group gains control over all money capital. Such a 'central bank' would thus exercise control over all social production.[45]

Capitalist development, in other words, tends ultimately towards the general cartel controlled by the central bank, a situation which Hilferding characterized as 'the consciously regulated society in antagonistic form'.[46]

For Hilferding then, class antagonism, instead of being reduced by the process of centralization, is actually heightened: an ever smaller number of economic rulers face an ever larger number of the economically dependent. As a result the mass of the population becomes ever more conscious of its class situation, finally gaining control of state power and hence control of the economy. The transition to socialism is made much easier by the progressive socialization of production that has already occured within capitalist relations:

> Once the proletarians have conquered the state, the state becomes the conscious organ of society. As soon as finance capital has brought under its control the most important branches of production, these become controlled by society the moment society has gained control of finance capital.... Today the expropriation of six large Berlin banks would mean the immediate expropriation of the most important areas of big industry and so long as capitalist forms of accounting still prove to be valuable, this would make it much easier to carry out socialist policy in the period of the transition to socialism.[47]

Quite clearly, Hilferding saw the epoch of finance capital as a specific phase of capitalist development. He therefore believed that the particular functions and laws of finance capital modified the inherent general laws of bourgeois society that Marx had worked out earlier. However, Hilferding explicitly understood his theory of finance capital not as a critique of Marxist theory but as a further development of it, legitimated by the empirical changes that had occured within capitalism.[49]

All the same, a comparison of certain aspects of Hilferding's theory with that of Marx shows that Hilferding's understanding of Marx is itself not unproblematic:

1 The first problem is the theory of centralization. For Marx centralization enables capitalists to expand the scale of their operations more rapidly than they can through 'normal' accumulation. Mergers make it possible for enormous capitals to be relatively quickly brought under a single control, the limit of centralization only being reached when within a given sector or a given society all capitals have been amalgamated into one single capital.[50] However, for Marx this is merely a logical possibility and centralization for him does not involve any qualitative alteration of the general laws of movement of capital: the centralized masses of capital 'reproduce and multiply as the others do, only more rapidly.'[51] Within the limits of capital's general laws of movement, capital centralized in the form of joint stock companies does however entail certain peculiarities: within the joint stock company disposal over capital is dissolved from private property so that the joint stock company is 'private production without private property'. Hence, Marx argues, in some circumstances the joint stock company can accumulate even if it has a lower rate of profit than other capitals, since instead of having to produce profit for the entrepreneur, it only needs to produce dividends as high as the current interest rate.[52] Engels's remarks on the question of centralization of capital go further than those of Marx: for him the trusts which grow out of the joint stock companies and which 'dominate and manage whole branches of industry' bring about not only 'the end of private production, but also the end of unplanned production.'[53]

An extensive degree of planning would in fact necessarily modify Marx's general laws of movement of capital, although it is unclear how great Engels believed the trusts' ability to plan actually was. Within his own discussion of the theory of centralization, Marx himself pointed out that in the transition from the capitalist mode of production to the associated mode of production advanced forms of the socialization of production such as the joint stock company and the credit system would be extremely important, although only as 'one element in connection with other great organic revolutions in the mode of production itself.'[54]

2 A second point of comparison between 'Finance Capital' and Marx's own theory is the theory of crisis and growth. Following Tugan-Baranowsky, Hilferding deduced capitalist development from Marx's reproduction schemata and in so doing fell into the same neo-equilibrium

interpretation.[55] For Hilferding the reproduction schemata contained the proof 'that in capitalist production both simple and expanded reproduction can occur without disturbance so long as these proportions [between the separate sectors of the economy] are kept the same.'[56] Consequently the basic reason for cyclical economic crises has to be seen in sectoral disproportionalities. From the claim that the problem of stabilization is essentially a question of coordinating numerous activities within the economy, Hilferding concludes that the tendency towards the centralization of economic decisions spells the possibility of harmonious accumulation even under capitalist conditions. This linkage of proportionality theory with cartel theory to prove that the capitalist system tends towards stabilization goes far beyond Tugan-Baranowsky's position, for the latter, almost anticipating later criticism of Hilferding's arguments, had explicitly warned against over-estimating the importance of cartels:

> A cartel can introduce planned organization of production within a single branch of industry, but the mutual relation of these planned branches of production remains just as unorganized and unplanned as before.[57]

3 Hilferding believed that Marx himself had anticipated his own central thesis of the domination of the banks over industry. Thus in his analysis of the circulation of capital Marx remarks that:

> as the scale of each individual process of production and with it the minimum size of the capital to be advanced increases in the process of capitalist production, we have here another circumstance to be added to those others which transform the functioning of the industrial capitalist more and more into a monopoly of big money-capitalists, who may operate singly or in association.[58]

Yet this statement really refers less to the relationship between industry and banks and far more to how capital is initially formed: while at the onset of industrialization the usual location of 'primary accumulation' was within craft production, over time capital formation became more and more the domain of the large capitalists.[59] Certainly, Marx was very far from believing that the contradictions of the capitalist mode of production could be overcome by changes in the circulation sphere: it is no accident that his criticisms of Saint-Simon's exaggerated belief in the banking system[60] can also be applied directly to Hilferding's belief in the all-pervasive planning power of finance capital.

Hilferding explicitly deduces his long-term predictions from his study of contemporary trends, and the fact that these predictions are faulty might naturally enough make one suspect the validity of his more short term analysis. However, this would be a mistake. Certainly, the thesis of finance capital as the domination of banks over industry was at the very least one-sided, even for Hilferding's own time – what were in fact historical peculiarities of the specific form in which capital had developed in Germany were elevated into features claimed as typical of capitalism as a whole. Nonetheless, this did not prevent Hilferding from developing a series of extremely fruitful insights into the way advanced capitalism functioned.

To mention only the most important:[61]

1 Hilferding investigated in detail the function and importance of paper money and began to free (even if not completely successfully) the Marxist theory of money from older metallist conceptions.[62]

2 Hilferding's theory of imperialism was a trailblazing contribution. Until his work, even within socialist thought imperialism had been considered as a primarily political occurance. Hilferding's own theory of imperialism, developed within the framework of his theory of finance capital, was the first step towards a materialist analysis, locating imperialism historically as 'the economic policy of finance capital'.[63] Thus he argued that as accumulation and centralization enormously enlarged the level of economic operations, it became advantageous and even necessary for finance capital increasingly to use the state apparatus to realize its own specific economic interests – against domestic competitors, in tariff policy and in overseas expansion. Capital accumulation went together with the growth in the export of capital, leading to a new phase in the relationship between the metropoles and colonies. In addition to the struggle for raw materials and markets there now appeared the struggle for spheres of influence for the capital which sought areas for investment. For the dependent countries capital import meant economic deformation which more than outweighed any expansionary effects it might have: the dependent economies were now linked to the metropoles as suppliers of cheap raw materials while the transfer of profits to the metropoles stopped any independent accumulation.

Hilferding's theory of imperialism also included an analysis of its social basis, examining the alliance between finance capital and large landowners, the importance of the 'declassed' petty bourgeois strata as a mass basis for imperialist policy and finally those effects of imperialism on working-class consciousness which were to be later discussed in terms of the theory of the 'labour aristocracy':

> The rapid increase in production also creates an increase in the demand for labour power, which in turn favours the trade unions; in the countries where capitalism first developed, its inherent tendencies towards the emiseration of the working class appear to have been overcome. The rapid growth of production prevents the injuries of capitalist society from coming to consciousness and makes for optimistic judgements of capitalism's ability to survive.[64]

5. Rosa Luxemburg: capital accumulation and imperialism

In Paul Mattick's striking formulation, it is quite possible to combine reformist practice with a revolutionary ideology, but it is hardly possible to carry out revolutionary practice with reformist theory.[65] Tugan-

Baranowsky initiated a tendency to use Marx's schemata of expanded reproduction to prove that capitalism could develop harmoniously and this claim amounted to a challenge to the radical wing of social democracy. It was to this problem of the possibilities of capitalist development which Rosa LUXEMBURG (1871–1919) devoted her study of the accumulation of capital. Starting from Marx's reproduction schemata, she investigated the general problem of capitalist reproduction as approached firstly within Marxist theory and secondly within bourgeois theory from Sismondi to Tugan-Baranowsky and the other representatives of Russian 'legal Marxism'. She thereby located an apparent inconsistency within Marxist theory which her own theoretical position was an attempt to resolve.

According to Rosa Luxemburg, while Marx's reproduction schemata are formally logical, they lead to misleading results. In that they assume accumulation for the sake of accumulation, they exclude the basic contradiction of capitalism – the contradiction between capitalism's ability to produce and its inability to consume.[67] That is to say, since it lies in the logic of the capitalist system to keep down the standard of living of the working class, capitalist society's ability to consume necessarily lags behind its ability to produce.

This inherent contradiction of capitalism means that if society consisted entirely of capitalists and wage-earners there would necessarily exist a structural lag of demand, the capitalists would be unable to realize their surplus value and accumulation would come to a halt. This does not happen for the sole reason that capitalists are able to dispose of part of their production outside this closed system of capital and wage labour, initially in their own country to the non-capitalist classes which still remain from the pre-capitalist period, and then increasingly in the non-capitalist colonies. If capital is to accumulate, it therefore needs a non-capitalist environment for investment and markets. However, the very process of investing and selling means that capitalism increasingly incorporates within itself this non-capitalist area. Sooner or later therefore the last hour of capitalism necessarily strikes, in theory at the latest when the last non-capitalist consumer is integrated into capitalism, but in practice however much earlier, because the intensified competition over the division of the world produces a chain of ever sharper economic and political crises. Rosa Luxemburg expressed the same ideas in the introduction to economics which grew out of the courses she taught at the SPD party school:

> The more capitalist production replaces less advanced forms of production, the more the necessity for profit limits the existing firms' ability to satisfy their need to expand their markets. One way of making this clear is to imagine for a moment that everything on the whole earth that was produced was produced capitalistically, that is to say, solely by private firms in large factories with modern wage workers. As soon as we do this, the impossibility of a permanent expansion of capitalism becomes clear.[68]

Despite its high level of abstraction, for Rosa Luxemburg herself the study was always meant to be of direct practical importance.[69] On this point at least her views were shared by all her critics within the SPD – the criticism her book received in the party press was in its form unusually harsh and in its content unusually wide ranging and hostile.[70] That not just theoretical issues were at stake was made clear in, for example, the conclusion of Eckstein's review:

> Once the theoretical assumptions are rejected, then so too must be the practical conclusions (above all the catastrophe theory) which comrade Luxemburg has erected on the basis of her thesis of the necessity of the non-capitalist countries for capitalism.[71]

Otto BAUER (1882–1938), like Eckstein an 'Austro-Marxist', responded to Rosa Luxemburg's accumulation theory with an extensive criticism, showing *inter alia* that even assuming an increasing organic composition of capital, it is still possible to calculate reproduction schemata which continue 'indefinitely'.[72] Despite their political affinities, her fellow left-wingers such as Pannekoek[73] and Lenin reacted equally negatively to her theory. Thus for example Lenin wrote:

> I have read Rosa's new book *Die Akkumulation des Kapitals*. She has got into a shocking muddle. She has distorted Marx. I am very glad that Pannekoek and Eckstein and O. Bauer have all with one accord condemned her, and said against her what I said in 1889 against the Narodniks.[74]

Lenin is quite justified in referring to the Russian debate on the capitalist market.[75] Rosa Luxemburg's theoretical starting point was the alleged discrepancy between the second and the third volumes of *Capital*, yet this discrepancy disappears the moment one realizes that the two theoretical arguments in the different volumes are also different methodologically – a point which Lenin had developed extensively in his controversy with the Narodniks and the legal Marxists. Marx's reproduction schemata are illustrations, constructed on the basis of arbitrary premises. Since they do not implicitly contain the general laws of movement of capital, they cannot be discussed in the same context as the theoretical arguments of the third volume. Since the alleged discrepancy is irrelevant, there is no need to attempt to overcome it by introducing additional theoretical arguments, as Rosa Luxemburg does with her *deus ex machina* of the non-capitalist areas. In that she accepts the neo-equilibrium interpretation that the formal structure of the reproduction schemata reflects the structure of the historical laws of movement of capital, Rosa Luxemburg's attempts to prove the collapse theory stand from the very beginning on unsure ground.

Nonetheless, Rosa Luxemburg's theory of accumulation is not irrelevant; it merits discussion because her focus on the realization problem is a focus on what is clearly a central problem of capitalist development. Manifestly however her attempts to solve the problem are misdirected. Marxist theory shows both that expanded reproduction is possible and that inherent in capitalism is the discrepancy between the ability to produce and the ability to consume. It is this discrepancy which is manifested in cyclical crises and which ultimately forms the historical limit of the capitalist mode of production: both the possibilities and the limits of capitalist accumulation can be explained from capital's inherent laws of movement, without the necessity of having recourse to the contingencies of capitalism's more or less complete geographical expansion.

6. Bukharin's theory of imperialism

During his years in exile from 1911 to 1917 Nikolai BUKHARIN (1888–1938) studied intensively the bourgeois economic theory of his time.[76] His critique of the marginal utility school[77] was extremely well received by Marxists and was considered worthy of attention by bourgeois writers as well.[78] Written in 1915, but only published after the October Revolution, his theory of imperialism is an important contribution to the further development of Marxist economics.[79]

Bukharin characterized the world economy in terms of the parallel internationalization and nationalization of capital. The internationalization of capital is the well known expansion of the capitalist world economy, accelerated from the end of the nineteenth century by capital mergers and international cartels, all of which Bukharin describes empirically in great detail. Parallel to this internationalization, there also occurs a process of nationalization of capital, i.e. the amalgamation of capital within national boundaries, and this follows just as necessarily as internationalization does from the general laws of movement of capital itself. Bukharin thus draws heavily on Hilferding's ideas for his initial theoretical assumption that concentration and centralization advance continually up to complete national organization. The thesis is best expressed in Bukharin's own words:

Where individual ownership of enterprises prevailed, individual capitalists opposed one another in the competitive struggle. At that time 'national economy' and 'world economy' were only sum totals of those comparatively small units that were interconnected by the circulation of commodities and competed with each other mainly within 'national' limits. The centralization process consisted in small capitalists being absorbed by large ones, in the growth of large-scale, individually owned, enterprises. With the growth of large-scale enterprises the extensive character of competition (within given territorial limits) decreased more and more; the number of competitors shrank with the growth of centralization. On the other hand, the intensity of the competition increased tremendously, for the smaller number of larger enterprises began to place on the market volumes of commodities unknown in former times. Concentration and centralization of capital finally brought about the formation of trusts. Competition rose to a still higher stage. Where formerly many individually owned enterprises competed with one another, there appeared the most stubborn competition between a few gigantic capitalist combines pursuing a complicated and, to a considerable degree, calculated policy. There finally comes a time when competition ceases in an entire branch of production. But the war for dividing up the surplus value between the syndicates of the various branches becomes fiercer; organizations producing manufactured goods arise against syndicates producing raw materials, and vice versa. The centralization process proceeds apace. Combines in industry and banking syndicates unite the entire 'national' production, which assumes the form of a company of companies, thus becoming a state capitalist trust. Competition reaches the highest, the last conceivable state of development. It is now the competition of state capitalist trusts in the world market.[80]

This passage is quoted here at length because it raises a problem that is central within theoretical discussion today, namely the role of the state in the process of the reproduction of capital. Obviously in Bukharin's 'state capitalism' the state is not an institution standing above the capital relation, it is not independent of the conflict between capital and labour; the state for Bukharin is dependent on the development of capital and has to be explained from it. The concentration and centralization of capital proceeds at first on the basis of the law of value, that is, on the basis of the economic superiority of the large firm. However, from a certain point on it becomes both possible and advantageous for the monopolies to strengthen their position by deliberately utilizing the power of the state as well as their immediate economic power. Historically this change occured together with the merger of industrial capital and banking capital into finance capital. Monopoly-controlled state intervention modifies the law of value in two ways. Firstly, and most importantly, on the international level the monopolies use the state against their foreign competitors, a process which began with the neo-protectionism of the 1880s; secondly, on a national level the state is also used against domestic competitors, especially the smaller and non-cartellized groups of the bourgeoisie. Bukharin analysed how this second process operates in particular during wartime – in the capitalist 'war economy'.[81] Like Hilferding, Bukharin considered that in their internal structure the state monopoly trusts represented the planning of production, even if this was still on the antagonistic basis of the opposition of capital and labour.

For Bukharin the process of centralization and concentration stops at the national borders – while Hilferding's 'general cartel' as the world-wide capitalist organization is certainly a possibility, this does not represent the real trend of socio-economic development. The reason lies in the uneven development of the capitalist countries in relation to each other. While capitalists may temporarily find international agreements beneficial, ultimately whichever group of them has the upper hand will prefer economically to subjugate the competing nation. Thus, while the anarchy of competition is overcome at the national level, at the international level it continues in a more acute form than ever, marked now by the massive use of state power. The logical results of such imperialist competition is world war.

The political conclusions of Bukharin's theory of imperialism are essentially directed against Kautsky's theory of 'ultra-imperialism'. Kautsky had claimed that the struggle between the imperialist powers over the mutual division of the world is followed by a period in which the imperialist nations renounce armed conflict and, cartel fashion, 'peacefully' distribute the world amongst themselves. Imperialism would then be replaced by ultra-imperialism.[82] Bukharin criticized this position as empirically false and politically reprehensible. Imperialist policy is not an act of will on the part of the bourgeoisie, but the logical consequence of capitalist development – accordingly the only historical alternative to aggressive imperialism is socialism. For Bukharin the imperialist war itself was acting to accelerate the transition to socialism. The working class of the advanced countries had been temporarily 'chained to the chariot of the bourgeois state power'[83] through its indirect share in the colonial extra-profits, but now, under the impact of the war, it was becoming aware of its class position.

As far as the question of international competition went, Lenin agreed with Bukharin's theory of imperialism.[84] He found less acceptable, however, the theory of state capitalism to which Bukharin remained committed in his later publications.[85] With his stress on the extent of planning and organization within capitalism, Bukharin essentially anticipated Hilferding's step from the theory of finance capitalism to that of 'organized capitalism'.[86] He thus laid himself open to the justifiable criticism that he ignored the basic regularities of the capitalist mode of production.

7. Lenin: imperialism is monopoly capitalism

Lenin's theory of imperialism has two basic elements which are already clear in his foreword to Bukharin's *Imperialism and the World Economy*: politically, the rejection of (to use a later term) the 'social imperialists' who tended to accommodate socialism to imperialism; theoretically, the understanding of capitalism as a special phase of capitalist development:

> At a definite stage in the development of exchange, at a definite stage in the growth of large-scale production, namely, at the stage which was attained towards the end of the century, exchange so internationalized economic relations and capital, and large-scale production assumed such proportions that monopoly began to replace free competition. Monopoly associations of entrepreneurs, trusts, instead of enterprises 'freely' competing with each other – at home *and in relations between the countries – became typical*.[88]

This idea is expressed in the now 'classic' formula in Lenin's study of imperialism itself:

> If it were necessary to give the briefest possible definition of imperialism we should have to say that imperialism is the monopoly stage of capitalism.[89]

Lenin fills out this definition by giving five basic characteristics of imperialism:

> (1) the concentration of production and capital has developed to such a high stage that it has created monopolies which play a decisive role in economic

life; (2) the merging of bank capital with industrial capital, and the creation on the basis of this 'finance capital' of a financial oligarchy; (3) the export of capital as distinguished from the export of commodities acquires exceptional importance; (4) the formation of international monopolist capitalist associations which share the world among themselves; and (5) the territorial division of the whole world amongst the biggest capitalist powers is completed.[90]

Lenin's conception of the process of centralization and concentration is very largely based on Hilferding's theory of finance capital; this is a debt which Lenin explicitly acknowledges[91] and it is demonstrated in Lenin's exhaustive analysis of Hilferding's book.[92] However, on two issues Lenin differs from Hilferding in ways which change his overall argument.

Firstly, Lenin uses Hilferding's concept of finance capital, but in so doing he stresses that the concentration of production towards monopoly is an independent development, separate to the centralization and dominating power of the banks:

> The concentration of production; the monopolies arising therefrom; the merging or coalescence of the banks with industry – such is the history of the rise of finance capital and such is the content of that concept.[93]

Secondly, Lenin argues with Hilferding in seeing monopoly capitalism as advancing the socialization of production, but unlike him, he stresses that the process occurs through contradictions. Thus the free competition amongst the small and medium-sized producers is superseded by another form of competition, that of monopolistic competition between the large firms. The keenness of this new competition is increased by the uneven development of the individual national economies on a world scale. These are the contradictions and the conflicts of the present to which the working class movement has to orientate itself, rather than basing its strategy, as Hilferding's arguments imply, on the theoretically conceivable but factually distant trend 'towards a single world trust absorbing all enterprises without exception and all states without exception.'[94]

Today discussion of Lenin's study is primarily concerned with the work's theoretical status and hence how it relates to Marx's work. If the latter is seen as being an analysis of the capitalist mode of production as a whole, then Lenin's theory of imperialism is only a concretization of Marx's basic theory. Alternatively, Marx's work can be seen merely as an analysis of the specific historical period of free competition, in which case it is replaced by Lenin's work since this must be assumed to analyse the new economic regularities of the new monopolist stage.[95] The discussion is stimulated by the fact that Lenin's own position on this question is extremely unclear. Initially Lenin says that the main task of his book is to give a 'composite picture'[96] of the capitalist world economy at the beginning of the twentieth century, and such a conception of its purpose fits the book's more descriptive than analytical form. Alternatively however, Lenin makes it clear that imperialism (or monopoly capitalism) counts for him as a special historical stage, clearly distinguished from that of competitive capitalism, being 'the transition from the capitalist system to a higher socio-economic order'[97] and having its own distinguishing characteristics: the widespread socialization of production, the partial replacement of economic laws by relations of direct domination, the long term weakening of profit-oriented accumulation (despite its initially so impressive growth) by the inherent tendency of monopoly capitalism towards parasitism, stagnation and decay. Lenin locates these characteristics in a purely descriptive fashion and does not go on from this to do what his argument implies he should, namely systematically to modify or even completely replace the laws of capitalism as Marx formulated them. The incomplete nature of Lenin's work is shown by the fact that the substance of the 'Leninist' theory of imperialism and monopoly capitalist was largely developed after Lenin's death.

At the time when Lenin formulated his theory of 'simple' monopoly capitalism the economic policy of the major capitalist countries in the first World War had already led to the merger of the economy and the state apparatus which Lenin later, in *State and Revolution*, was to term state monopoly capitalism. Its three defining characteristics were the enormous growth of the state machinery, the merger of the state machinery with the large capitalist groups and,. as far as the situation of the working class was concerned, 'military discipline for the workers.'[98] According to Lenin state monopoly capitalism is a necessary development of 'simple' monopoly capitalism, although he held that the war had 'greatly accelerated'[99] this change. As Lenin was to argue in relation to Russian conditions, state monopoly capitalism represented the furthest socialization of production possible under capitalist conditions. State monopoly capitalism therefore formed the initial material basis for socialism:

> Socialism is merely the next step forward from state capitalist monopoly. Or, in other words, socialism is merely state capitalist monopoly *which is made to serve the interests of the whole people* and has to that extent *ceased* to be capitalist monopoly.[100]

In the theory of state monopoly capitalism, even more so than in the theory of imperialism, Lenin defines a historical stage of capitalism by particular 'exemplary' historical phenomena (here the involvement of the state apparatus in the reproduction process of capital). Certainly, in his focus on the involvement of the state in the economy, Lenin hit on a trend which is basic in capitalism; given that many people believed that the war economy represented a form of socialism ('war socialism'), Lenin's conceptual location of state intervention within the general framework of monopoly capitalism was important both theoretically and politically. Nonetheless, it is still a matter of debate whether Lenin's theory of state monopoly capitalism can be generalized from this particular historical situation into the core of a general theory of a particular stage of capitalism as a whole. Lenin considered state monopoly capitalism, as concretely manifested in the war economy, as the final stage of capitalism. Consequently when, after 1918, in the major capitalist countries the war economy was dismantled and economic controls removed, the concept of state monopoly capitalism immediately lost its empirical basis. It is no accident that in the Comintern's analysis of capitalism the concept plays no role; equally consistently, modern advocates of the theory of state monopoly capitalism are forced to bring all state activity in the 1920s under the rather arbitrary label of 'state monopoly capitalism'. Finally, if state monopoly capitalism is defined as the final stage of capitalism, the whole concept becomes theoretically meaningless once this 'final stage' is continually and indefinitely prolonged:

> More than 50 years ago V.I. Lenin characterized state monopoly capitalism as the complete material preparation for socialism. Today, when state monopoly capitalism has expanded so extensively, this finding is more relevant then ever before.[102]

And how much more, one could add, will the finding apply in another 50 years! Used like this, state monopoly capitalism applies to every situation after 1917 and so characterizes none of them.

4

THEORIES OF CAPITALISM FROM THE OCTOBER REVOLUTION TO THE PRESENT DAY

1. The general crisis of capitalism: the Comintern's analysis of capitalism

With the Russian Revolution of October 1917 the world economy was divided into two competing economic systems; at the same time the working-class movement was split into revolutionary and reformist wings. Up until the first World War these two wings had institutionally at least been united under the roof of the Second International, now in 1919 they reconstituted themselves as the new Second International and the Communist Third International respectively. One way in which this split was expressed was in divergent theoretical views on the economic stability of capitalism.

In March 1919 the Communist International held its first congress. The new International based itself on the assumption that the class struggle was now entering 'the epoch of the final decisive battle.'[1] This claim was justified by an economic analysis based on the immediate experience of the war economy and the situation directly after the war. For the Comintern there were three crucial aspects to the new period. First, during the war the living conditions of the masses had enormously deteriorated. Secondly, the war was seen as having led to the merger of the state and the economy: in describing this as 'the nationalization of economic life'[2] the Comintern came close to Lenin's concept of state monopoly capitalism, without however explicitly using the term. Finance capital, so the Communist International argued, could now only fulfil its economic functions 'by means of blood and iron.'[3] Thirdly, the geographical area of capitalist rule had been reduced, due to the October Revolution in Russia and the liberation movements in the colonies which were taking on a social as well as a national character. The world economic crisis of 1921 only served to strengthen this belief in the imminent collapse of capitalism. For example, in VARGA's interpretation the crisis of 1921 is no normal crisis of overproduction, but instead is the signal that capitalism is entering a long crisis-ridden final phase:

> The periods of economic upswing grow shorter and shorter, the crises become ever longer and ever deeper; more and more countries are dragged into the

general decay; the revolutionary movement of the working class pushes capitalism into ever more crises, until finally after long struggles the social revolution finally triumphs.[5]

For Varga one basic aspect of the crisis was the narrowing of the world market. This was seen as being the result of both the Russian Revolution and also of the fact that Central Europe had been so impoverished that it too was effectively eliminated from the world market. The reduction of the world market also exacerbated the crisis indirectly, for it would inevitably force the remaining imperialist world powers into a new world war, this time between Great Britain and the United States.

Despite its broad claims, Varga's analysis, just like the theses of the Comintern, remains restricted to the level of the immediate appearance of the economic situation. Further, economic analysis is here subordinated to directly political considerations, as is shown not least by the fact that Varga and the Comintern are only able to understand the world market in purely geographical terms.

Contrary to what the revolutionaries expected, outside Russia capitalism was able politically to consolidate itself: the international monetary system was stabilized, if only for a short period, and material reproduction reached and even surpassed pre-war levels. In 1924 at its fifth congress the Comintern acknowledged that these limited tendencies towards stabilization did exist, but this recognition then sat rather uneasily with its insistence that the general crisis of capitalism was still deepening:

> The ruin of the capitalist world economy has greatly advanced in many of the most important capitalist countries. While the capitalist offensive is able to create a temporary respite for individual capitalist groups and individual capitalist states, it simultaneously also sharpens the contradictions between these same groups and states.[6]

This is the outline of the thesis of the 'relative stabilization of capitalism' which was to become the official position of the Communist International.[7] While in Marx's theory 'crisis' meant a fairly regular cyclical event, now the term is used here to mean a longer period of latent instability. It is in this sense for example that Varga juxtaposes the two concepts of 'the general crisis of capitalism' and 'the final period of capitalism':

> What is meant by a period of crisis? By a period of crisis we mean a general condition of capitalist society in which the forces of production have developed to about the highest possible level which they can within this form of society; at the same time the internal contradictions of capitalism are so deep, the class contradictions objectively so sharp, and the power apparatus of the ruling classes has been so weakened, that it is objectively possible for the rule of the bourgeoisie to be overthrown and the struggle for the dictatorship of the proletariat to be victorious. Obviously, the crisis period does not mean that any attempt to sieze power anywhere and at any time always has the possibility of being successful. Equally, the period of crisis does not mean that

the subjective and objective conditions are always unfavourable and always similar. For this reason, in order to make clear that the period of crisis is a drawn out period, I have also used the term 'period of decline' to describe this period.[8]

The thesis of relative stabilization was in 1926 defended by Bukharin on two fronts. On the one side he attacked contemporary social democratic theory. Frequently using the concept of 'organized capitalism', social democratic theorists of the time argued that capitalism was developing in a way which now made possible a non-revolutionary evolution towards socialism: the capitalist order had now been consolidated so that there was the prospect of an approaching capitalist prosperity, the anarchy of capitalism had been overcome both internationally and nationally, while finally the basic power relationships within capitalist society had changed. On the other side, Bukharin attacked the left-wing theorists, such as Trotsky and Zinoviev, who denied that even a relative stabilization had occurred. Bukharin demonstrated empirically that there was a tendency towards relative stabilization, without however discussing it more closely in theoretical terms. Stabilization for Bukharin was 'relative' for three reasons. Firstly, the extent of the capitalist world market had been reduced by the October Revolution in Russia, by the beginnings of the socialist movement in China and by the decline of the British Empire. Secondly, the process of emiseration which had begun during the war had drastically cut the standard of living of the masses. Using very similar arguments to those used by Varga in 1921, Bukharin saw the enormous income disparities which stemmed from the war as the immediate cause of the crisis which could be observed in some countries in 1925/26. Thirdly, stabilization was relative because it was not based on any economic regularities but only on the deliberate intervention of the state apparatus in the economic process.

The increased activity of the state which Bukharin noticed was analysed in more detail by Varga under the term of 'state capitalism'. By this Varga at first meant the independent economic activity of the state, as opposed to its more general regulation of the economy, and he only defined the term more broadly after the experience of the world economic crisis of 1929–1933:

> The main result of the attempts to artificially overcome the crisis, as indeed of the whole of capitalist economic policy during the crisis, has been the intervention of the state into the most detailed workings of the economy. This intervention is an intervention in favour of the ruling classes in general and in favour of monopoly capitalism and the large landowners in particular .... The 'state capitalist' tendencies receive a strong impetus; to a certain extent there is a transition from monopoly capitalism to a 'state war-monopoly-capitalism', as Lenin called capitalism in the period of the world war.[11]

As specific elements of state capitalism Varga named the relative increase of state expenditure, the regulation of foreign trade, job creation and labour service together with state control of prices and of the banks.[12] More than Lenin's original concept of state monopoly capitalism, Varga's concept of state capitalism in many respects anticipates the contemporary theory of state monopoly capitalism. However, since Varga restricts himself merely to describing the different measures of state intervention and does not show the relationship between the different economic functions of the state, he does not provide much basis for determining the possibilities and the limits of state intervention.

In retrospect the concept of 'relative stabilization' compares favourably to its social democratic contemporaries. Social democratic theory, like bourgeois economics, expected a permanent prosperity within capitalism. Yet accurate observation does not amount to systematic theory – the Comintern's analysis of capitalism clearly limited itself merely to describing various surface aspects of the capitalist world economy. Thus, concepts such as 'the general crisis', 'the final phase' and 'relative stabilization' are all terms which are more strategic political descriptions of capitalism than the basis of any economic analysis. In fact, more successful than this attempt fully to grasp a new period of capitalist development conceptually was the application of Marxist theory to the concrete description of economic events: the quarterly analyses of the economic situation which Varga published from 1922 on in *Inprecorr* compare extremely favourably to the official bourgeois analyses,[13] even though these were carried out with much larger resources.[14]

2. 'Organized capitalism' as the core of reformist theory

In his introduction to 'Finance Capital' Hilferding developed the idea that Marxist political economy has no necessary link with the working class. If this were so, then potentially at least Marxist theory could be separated from the working-class movement and used completely instrumentally by any decision-makers who wished to do so:

> Marxism provides an insight into the laws of movement of society and those who have this insight always have the advantage.[15]

The validity of this belief is challenged by the actual policy of the social democratic parties wherever they held government power in the 1920s and 1930s. In many cases the social democrats renounced any specifically socialist economic theory and, faced with the need to make concrete decisions, acted according to the prescriptions of bourgeois economic theory: the resulting policies were just as successful (as in Sweden) or just as unsuccessful (as in Great Britain) as those of bourgeois governments.[16] In the countries where there was still a strong Marxist tradition, everyday social democratic policy still had to be legitimated by a Marxist theory, and it is in this respect that the theory of 'organized capitalism' is interesting.

The theory of 'organized capitalism' was developed by Rudolf Hilferding to characterize the socio-economic changes which had occurred during the first World War.[17] The notion of 'organization' itself was prevalent not only within Germany. For example, independently of Hilferding's theory, the French right-wing socialists developed the concept of an 'organized economy'.[18] Unlike Lenin, Hilferding saw the direct involvement of the state in the reproduction process of capital not as the expression of the ever deepening contradictions of capitalism, but as a step towards the long term stabilization of the capitalist mode of production.[19] Organized capitalism appeared to him to be completely conceivable as an historical alternative to socialism:

> Instead of socialism being victorious, a society could develop with an organized but nonetheless hierarchical and undemocratic economy. At the head of this economy would stand the united powers of the capitalist monopolies and the state; beneath them would be the masses, organized in hierarchical ranks as officials of production. Instead, therefore, of capitalist society being abolished, a form of capitalism would develop which would be better adapted to the immediate needs of the masses than capitalism has been up to now.[20]

In the course of developing his theory of organized capitalism after the relative stabilization of the 1920s, Hilferding somewhat altered his original position: instead of being as an historical alternative to socialism, organized capitalism now appeared as a transitional stage along the route to it.[21] The defining characteristics of this organized capitalism were:

1 technical progress in general and in particular the utilization of chemistry, since the latter made production independent of natural raw materials;

2 the organization of the economy into trusts and cartels;

3 internationalization;

4 the gradual replacement of free competition by the planned administration of society: 'In reality therefore organized capitalism means the replacement of the capitalist principle of free competition by the socialist principle of planned production.'[22] At the concrete politico-economic level the equivalent to the theoretical concept of organized capitalism was the idea of 'economic democracy'. This expressed a programme of democratic control of the economy through workers' participation. Just like 'organized capitalism', 'economic democracy' was seen as ultimately leading to the final goal of socialism.[23]

The original theory of finance capitalism had already contained a harmonious conception of how capitalist development would end. The theory of organized capitalism developed this conception more forcefully and applied it to the political present: the new theory was not so much the expression of a Marxist orientation as of the need for a Marxist gloss for social democratic policy. How far social democratic politics had become separated from socialist theory was made clear in 1918. Completely rejecting the position he himself had adopted in *Das Finanzkapital*, Hilferding now explicitly opposed any socialization of the banks and generally advocated a very leisurely tempo of socialization.[24] As the central concept of reformism, organized capitalism was meant to provide a legitimation in terms of Marxist theory for the policy of the SPD at national, state and local level. The consequences clearly amounted to complete reformism. Marxist theory was now only a rhetorical reference point – for concrete analysis social democracy relied on bourgeois economics. This applied particularly to Hilferding himself, who consequently made drastic mistakes on virtually every relevant economic question of the time: on structural unemployment in the 1920s, on the outbreak of the world economic crisis and finally on stabilization policy.[25] In a time of wars and crises the theory of organized capitalism of necessity could only disorientate its adherents. Recently some historians do seem to have found the theory of organized capitalism to be of some use as a way of summarizing the structural changes which have occurred since the end of the nineteenth century in the economy and in society as a whole. However, used like this the theory of organized capitalism is no longer recognizable as a specifically socialist theory, nor is it intended to be one.[26]

3. Once again: the accumulation of capital

During the 1920s and on the fringes of political discussion the old controversy continued between 'neo-equilibrium theorists' and 'collapse theorists' on the implications of Marx's reproduction schemata for the theory of economic growth. On the reformist side, Rudolf Hilferding reaffirmed his neo-equilibrium theory of development which had now become one of the theoretical pillars of the theory of organized capitalism. Hilferding's comments at a congress of the Verein für Sozialpolitik show how he continued to connect an analysis of expanded reproduction with a belief in capitalism's economic stability:

> I am convinced that this view of mine completely accords with the teachings of Karl Marx, who is always falsely claimed to have held a collapse theory of capitalism. Precisely the second volume of *Capital* shows how it is possible for production within the capitalist system to continue at ever higher levels. I have often thought that it is really no such terrible thing that this second volume is so rarely read, because it could, under certain conditions, be interpreted as a hymn of praise to capitalism.[27]

During the early 1920s there was no discussion of the theory of capitalist development within the left wing of the socialist movement. This was a neglect which Bukharin made up for in 1925 with an extensive criticism of Rosa Luxemburg's work.[28] Like Lenin before him, Bukharin defended Marx against Luxemburg's misunderstandings of him and stressed the analytical value of the reproduction schemata. For Bukharin, the reproduction schemata are an analytical instrument which can be applied both to a process of planned economic growth under capitalist conditions ('state capitalism') and to socialist accumulation.[29] Methodologically,

Bukharin's use of the reproduction schemata is an advance. Even if it is not completely satisfactory, it does at least show that discussion of the reproduction schemata need not rely, as it usually does, on laborious and often confusing mathematical calculations.[30]

Independent of one another, Fritz Sternberg and Henryk Grossman both developed their own attempts to deduce conclusively the collapse of the capitalist system from the reproduction schemata. In his theory of imperialism and capitalist collapse Fritz STERNBERG (1895–1963) accepted Rosa Luxemburg's view that

> imperialism, i.e. the expansion of capitalism into non-capitalist territories, is an inherent necessity of capitalism; for should capitalism be not merely the dominant economic form but the sole economic form, then in a very short time it would have to disintegrate under its own economic contradictions.[31]

Sternberg justifies his collapse theory by linking theoretically imperialism with the reproduction schemata, but in a way which diverges from Rosa Luxemburg's own theory of imperialism.

According to Sternberg, the advance of capitalism into non-capitalist areas not only opens up new possibilities for exports, but is also simultaneously a precondition for a rise in real wages within the capitalist countries. Imperialism thus indirectly creates an expansion of the domestic market. Sternberg justifies this claim with a wage theory taken from Franz Oppenheimer: the 'surplus population', the fact that 'two workers chase after every employer'[32] is a precondition for the capitalists' being able to gain any surplus value at all, and how high the wages of labour are at any one moment depends upon the pressure of the surplus population. The imperialist expansion of the second half of the nineteenth century occurred at a time when in the metropoles the pre-capitalist strata had been largely obliterated, and so were no longer a possible source of surplus population. Simultaneously, since the export of capital means that the organic composition of capital increased more slowly than previously, capitalism's inherent tendency continually to expel labour from the production process also declined. Therefore imperialism meant that while the chances of capitalist expansion increased, at the same time the pressure of the surplus population declined and consequently the wages of labour could rise.

This 'golden age' of capitalism could not however last for long. Sternberg argued that the extent of the non-capitalist areas still to be opened up was rapidly declining, all the more so because the expansion of capitalism itself was turning ever more 'passively imperialist' countries into 'actively imperialist' ones which were themselves beginning to compete with the older metropoles. As for Lenin, for Sternberg the first World War was an imperialist war over the division of the world; with the end of the 'golden age' because of the end of capitalism's territorial expansion, the war could only be followed by a chain of ever acuter crises and further wars. Sternberg supplements his economic analysis with a theory of revolution which is in fact more of a cultural criticism than an economic theory: without socialist revolution, wars and crises are inevitable and their consequence will be the decline of Europe into an undefined 'historylessness'.[33]

Sternberg's attempt to use a theory of wages to prove that capitalism's development depends on the existence of non-capitalist areas must be considered a failure.[34] On the question of markets Sternberg falls into exactly the same misunderstanding of the reproduction schemata as Rosa Luxemburg does, while his use of Oppenheimer's wage theory does not solve the problem but merely leads to additional errors, of which the first is a striking misunderstanding of, or even ignorance of, Marx's theory of surplus value. It is no accident that Sternberg's later publications on imperialism are more descriptive than analytical.[35]

From the Russian revisionism debate to Sternberg the discussion of Marx's reproduction schemata focused on the realization of surplus value. Marx's argument assumes a growing mass of surplus value, and the question then becomes whether and how this surplus value can be realized. By contrast, in his version of the collapse theory Henryk GROSSMANN (1881–1950) stands the problem on its head. For Grossmann 'the surplus value is not sufficient for accumulation to continue at the given rate of accumulation! Hence the catastrophe.'[36] This thesis is the core of Grossmann's theory and despite the length of Grossmann's work, its proof is surprisingly simple.

Grossmann starts from the reproduction schema which Otto Bauer had developed in his criticism of Rosa Luxemburg shortly before the first World War.[37] Bauer was able to show that it is possible to calculate a continuing and trouble-free accumulation of capital over a number of periods, even given a rising organic composition of capital. Bauer believed that this finally provided a firm basis for the neo-equilibrium interpretation of Marx's reproduction schemata, but what he did not notice is that in the long term his assumptions lead to a rather remarkable result. If the organic composition of capital rises and the rate of surplus value stays constant, then obviously the ratio of constant capital to surplus value also continually rises. If one then follows the model's assumptions and allows constant capital to grow at a constant rate, then sooner or later a point will be reached at which the mass of surplus value from the current period is smaller than the amount of capital which, according to the assumptions, has to be invested to maintain the rate of growth. Grossmann calculated that, taking the figures used by Bauer in his reproduction schema, from the thirty-eighth period on accumulation collapses for lack of surplus value. With 'a breathtaking mental leap'[38] Grossmann translates the laws of Bauer's reproduction schema into the laws of capitalist development, concluding that just like the theoretical model, the capitalist system itself would collapse for lack of sufficient surplus value. With some modifications this collapse is made to yield a theory of crisis: 'realistically' Grossmann expects the collapse not after thirty-five years, but after the length of a normal period of economic upturn. In the crises capital is then periodically devalued, thus reducing the amount of new capital needed for investment, and the accumulation process can begin again once more. Nonetheless, since in each crisis the average amount of capital tends to increase, the final collapse remains unavoidable.

Grossmann's theory is a theory of over-accumulation. However, for Grossmann the reason over-accumulation slows down capitalist development is not a fall in the rate of profit, but the growing discrepancy between the amount of capital needed for accumulation and the total mass of profits (the amount of capital needed for accumulation is treated as being determined by the initial conditions in each cycle of reproduction and by the assumed constant rate of growth of capital). Implicitly the theory does include the tendency of the rate of profit to fall, since it assumes an increasing organic composition of capital and a constant rate of exploitation. Nonetheless, the profit rate for Grossmann is merely a coefficient and has no independent meaning for the dynamic development of the system. Consequently, Grossmann effectively replaces the rate of profit in Marx's accumulation theory with the mass of profit.[39]

By itself the fact that Grossmann sees himself forced simply to rewrite Marx's text at important points shows a certain contradiction between his conclusions and his original intention of merely adequately reconstructing Marx's theory of crisis and collapse and purging it of earlier writers' false interpretations. Clearly, Grossmann can only argue that accumulation can catch up and 'overtake' the amount of available surplus value because he has beforehand fixed an arbitrary rate of accumulation, without considering at all the development of the profit rate and employers' investment decisions. Depending on what initial assumptions are made, a procedure like this can just as plausibly produce calculations which demonstrate capitalism's long term stability as calculations which demonstrate the inevitability of the ultimate collapse of capitalism. The interrelationships between the different macro-economic aggregates, the question of what forms of economic behaviour stand behind the individual components of the overall macro-economic calculations – all this is simply ignored by Grossmann. In Sweezy's formulation, Grossman's theory reveals extremely clearly 'the danger of mechanistic thinking in the social sciences',[40] and in particular, the banality of the very long theoretical tradition based on the calculation of the reproduction schemata – its formalism makes it impossible for it to lead to any understanding of Marx's theory of accumulation and of the real process of accumulation.[41] It is therefore not as astonishing as it at first appears that Grossmann could publish his book on the collapse of the capitalist system in 1929 without making any reference at all to the real class struggles of his time, including even those of the October Revolution.[42]

Grossman's study marks the end of the discussion based around the reproduction schemata. This is partly for reasons which have nothing to do with the debate itself (the 1930s, as is well known, were hardly a favourable time for theoretical work), but in many ways the nature of the subject ensured that the exhaustive discussion did not produce any further theoretical advances. Hence the systematic summaries of the controversies by Natalie Moskowska in the 1930s and by Paul Sweezy later are also, so it seems, conclusions to the discussion.[43]

4. Neo-Marxism

The label 'neo-Marxism' is partly an expression of the difficulty of finding a common theme which unites the theorists from outside the socialist countries who are discussed in the rest of this chapter.[44] Nevertheless, despite the lack of a debate in the sense of a direct exchange of arguments, these theorists do have enough in common both methodologically and in terms of their social position to form an identifiable current. They all share the belief that the theoretical impulses of the Second and Third International are now exhausted and that the theoretical stagnation can only be overcome by new approaches which involve both a direct return to Marx and a direct confrontation with bourgeois theory. They are also united by the fact that although their theoretical work takes issue with the big organizations of the working class movement and with the transitional socialist societies, institutionally it is separated from both of these, in so far as these writers have any connection with the organized working-class movement it is through organizations which are politically essentially marginal groups.

The bridge between the 1930s and the 1960s is shown most clearly in Paul Sweezy's *The Theory of Capitalist Development*.[45] When it was published in 1942 the first edition was intended to acquaint American readers with what was then contemporary European Marxist theory. The German edition of 1959 was published at the beginning (or just before the beginning) of the rebirth of Marxism in Germany; it made available to the German reader a theoretical tradition which had been very largely produced in German-speaking areas and then subsequently effectively suppressed by fascism and the post-war restoration. As an analytical and exhaustive resume of the history of Marxist theory up to the 1930s, Sweezy's book is still without any rivals today. More than this, Sweezy develops his own position on the theory of crisis and accumulation. Although its conclusions are still disputed, Sweezy's argument here places Marx's original method at the centre of the analysis, unlike the earlier distortions of the reproduction-schema theorists and of the Comintern and its need for self-justification.

For Sweezy Marx's method means not just the work of the master himself, but also its subsequent development in particular by Lenin, who is central for Sweezy in two ways: firstly, the linkage of disproportionality and crisis ('theory of the markets')[46] developed in the Russian revisionism debate, and secondly the definition of contemporary capitalism as monopoly capitalism. Sweezy's own theory of monopoly capitalism is an attempt to deduce, more systematically than had been done before, the phenomena of contemporary capitalism from inherent economic laws.

1 Since monopoly increases the profit rate of individual capitals, but not the profit rate in the economy as a whole, extra profit is only made at the expense of non-monopolized firms. Monopoly therefore works against the equalization of the profit rate which is assumed to occur under competitive conditions. Since monopolization advances at a different speed in the different sectors of the economy, a 'hierarchy of profit rates' is formed, 'ranging from the highest in the industries of large-scale production where close well-protected combinations are relatively easy to establish, to the lowest in the industries of very small-scale production where numerous firms coexist and the ease of entry precludes stable combinations.'[47]

2 Precisely where profit is concentrated, there the inherent nature of monopoly results in a slowing down of accumulation. Monopolization restricts each individual monopoly's accumulation, firstly because once the monopoly has achieved an optimal market and price situation, any further accumulation and expansion of production would reduce its total profits, secondly, because when the monopolist considers investing in technical innovations he must take into account that this will devalue the capital he has already invested.

3 Monopolization leads to realization difficulties and tendencies towards stagnation. Temporarily at least these can be compensated for by capital being absorbed through the expansion of the marketing and distribution apparatus beyond the level which is socially necessary. Hence contempory capitalism takes the form of waste capitalism: it can only survive because it directs the forces of production into socially unnecessary areas.

The core of Sweezy's argument is that monopolization slows down accumulation. Given his assumption of static market behaviour on the part of monopolies this appears plausible enough, but the argument appears more debatable the moment one considers the more general (and just as realistic) case where the monopolist not only extracts his extra profits from existing markets, but also is able to use innovation and accumulation to create new markets. Despite Sweezy's arguments then, accumulation can be rational even under monopolistic conditions.

Sweezy's theory of monopoly capitalism is developed further in *Monopoly Capital*, a book which resulted from many years of joint work with Paul Baran and which leads directly into present day discussion.[48] The central theme of the study is the 'generation and absorption of surplus under conditions of monopoly capitalism',[49] documented empirically through the example of the most advanced capitalist country, the USA. The concept of 'surplus' here corresponds to Baran's earlier concept of surplus as 'the potential economic surplus', defined by Baran as:

> the difference between the output that *could* be produced in a given natural and technical environment with the help of employable production resources, and what might be regarded as essential consumption.[50]

The 'potential economic surplus' then is not derived directly from the process of capital valorization (as is for example Marx's concept of surplus value), but instead is a category determined according to the criterion of social use value by an observer who stands to a certain extent outside the relations of production. The same applies to Baran's concept of surplus:

> The economic surplus, in the briefest possible definition, is the difference between what society produces and the costs of producing it. The size of the surplus is an index of productivity and wealth, of how much freedom a society has to accomplish whatever goals it may set for itself.[51]

Concretely, property incomes, state expenditure and waste in the economic process comprise the main components of the surplus, and surplus for Baran and Sweezy is the key category for understanding contemporary capitalism. As monopoly capitalism the capitalism of today is distinguished clearly from the competitive capitalism of Marx's time, basically for two reasons. Firstly, under conditions of monopoly capitalism the surplus increases both absolutely and in relation to total production; secondly, within this system the growing surplus is not invested in a way which is rational for society as a whole, but instead is absorbed in multifarious forms of waste. The category of surplus is a concentrated expression of the contradictions of contemporary capitalism which Sweezy had located already in his *The Theory of Capitalist Development*: the price of capitalism's development of the forces of production is their increasingly irrational application.

At first sight the 'law of increasing surplus' appears to contradict Marx's theorem of the tendency of the rate of profit to fall. Baran and Sweezy themselves certainly see their 'law' in this way, explaining their revision of Marx's theory by the transition from competitive capitalism to monopoly capitalism. However, Baran and Sweezy do not in fact bring Marx's theory of accumulation up to date, but instead produce a completely different theory with a different method and a different object.[52] Baran's original concept of the 'potential economic surplus' had been extremely useful, particularly in the discussion of 'development theory', where it could be used to show that despite arguments based on the alleged 'vicious circle of poverty', the ability of the 'developing' countries to accumulate depends in the first instance on the relations of production and not on the forces of production, i.e. the problem is how the economic surplus can be rationally used instead of being allowed to be squandered on luxury consumption. In the same way the notion of surplus illustrates particular phenomena of contemporary capitalism which are, on plausible social criteria, an irrational waste of productive ability. However, all of this has basically very little to do with Marx's political economy, and for Baran and Sweezy the historical limit of capitalism is not a question of the dynamics of social classes and the class struggle, but a question of moral appeals and of 'reasonable' reflection by rational individuals. It was in fact precisely in this way that *Monopoly Capital* was so important for the neo-

Marxist renaissance of the 1960s, which was (and to a large extent still is) a revolt of the 'socially aware' outside the class struggle itself.[53]

Apart from its initial effects, *Monopoly Capital* was not a stage in the development of socialist economic theory which could lead on to further advances. In a certain sense contemporary neo-Marxist theory begins at the beginning – on the one hand by returning directly to the 'classics', on the other hand by confronting the theories of capitalism which have been produced in the socialist countries.[54]

5. The theory of state monopoly capitalism

One all too obvious effect of Stalinism was that it did not exactly encourage the development of socialist theory. As formulated for example by Stalin in his comments on the draft of a new textbook of political economy,[55] the official Soviet analysis of capitalism essentially repeated the analysis put forward by the Comintern in its early period. If anything, even more than the Comintern, these official analyses stressed that capitalism is of its nature inherently crisis-ridden and that its ultimate demise is imminent.

1   The general crisis of capitalism is accentuated by the collapse of a unitary world market.

2   Average profits or even temporary extra-profits are no longer enough to satisfy the monopolies, who now only invest when they are enticed to do so by 'maximal profit' (something which is never defined more exactly). Since this maximal profit by definition only occurs very rarely, increasingly expanded reproduction in monopoly capitalism will slow down. Stalin thus explicitly rejects his previous thesis of the 'relative stability of the markets' as well as Lenin's thesis that despite the general decay of capitalism, its actual growth is by and large considerably faster than before.[56]

3   Further wars between the capitalist countries are inevitable.

4   Stalin anticipates a central point of the more recent theory of 'state monopoly capitalism' (the 'stamocap' theory as it is sometimes known) with his formula of 'the subordination of the state apparatus to the monopolies';[57] he does not however examine in any more detail how this control actually occurs.

In line with the custom of the period, Stalin's remarks became the obligatory basis for any analysis of capitalism, as can be seen for example in Varga's extensive discussion of imperialism.[58] Varga repeats the thesis of the further deepening of the general crisis, maximal profit, the inevitability of new imperialist wars. Hence his conclusion:

> Thus the new stage of the general crisis of capitalism is characterized above all by the formation of two camps and two parallel world markets – the capitalist market, becoming smaller every day, and the socialist world market, expanding rapidly and systematically. The laws of decaying capitalism lead inevitably to the sharpening of all of capitalism's contradictions, to economic chaos and to crises of over-production, to the emiseration of the broadest

masses of the working people, to chronic mass unemployment, to reaction and to fascism.[59]

What is provided here is basically not an economic theory at all. Instead Varga is formulating a political prediction, or to be more precise (and as became more and more obvious as time went on) a political hope, which could be expressed *inter alia* in economic concepts.

Given the high rates of economic growth and the levelling out of the business cycle in the capitalist countries, in the long term it was impossible to maintain this belief that the immediate post war period would be one of major economic crisis. The destalinization of the middle 1950s therefore enabled a revision of the official theory of capitalism which was long overdue. In the second half of the decade there appeared a series of important empirical investigations of the changes in the business cycle.[60] Parallel to these, the works of KUSMINOV and GLUSCHKOW in the Soviet Union[62] and Kurt ZIESCHANG in the German Democratic Republic[62] initiated a new theoretical orientation, centred around the concept of 'state monopoly capitalism'.

This notion had been used by Lenin to characterize certain phenomena of the war economy on the basis of his general theory of imperialism and monopoly capitalism. After the First World War the term disappeared from Marxist discussion[63] and only re-emerged after the Second World War. In 1947 the Soviet economist N.M. Smit recalled in a discussion with Varga that Lenin had defined contemporary capitalism as state monopoly capitalism, a phase which had superseded monopoly capitalism during the First World War; Smit claimed that this state monopoly capitalism had developed further as a result of the Second World War.[64] Hence Smit criticized Varga for terming Lenin's concept 'state war monopoly capitalism' and only applying it to the specific form of the capitalist economy in wartime.[65] In the GDR the notion of state monopoly capitalism began to be used to describe particular forms of state intervention, although at first no broader theoretical claims were made for the concept and there was no confrontation with Lenin's original concept.[66] The idea of state monopoly capitalism was now present again in Marxist discussion, but its vagueness allowed it to be used relatively freely. This was the situation in the middle of the 1960s when some theorists began to analyze contemporary capitalism systematically as state monopoly capitalism.

For Zeischang the contradictions of capitalist development become sharper in the stage of state monopoly capitalism, but at the same time new mechanisms of stabilization develop. As a result the tendency towards economic collapse is weakened, even though it is impossible for it to be removed altogether. The central point is the involvement of the state in the process of capital reproduction – an involvement which is deduced from the tendency towards the concentration of capital: after capital has reached a certain size investments, production and capital valorization have to be secured by the state. In addition, the big corporations become so important in relation to society as a whole that the stability of the system in general becomes interlocked with the economic stability of the individual corporation. In Zeischang's argument the development of capitalism is shaped more by these internal factors than by the system competition between the capitalist and the socialist societies.

Zieschang was the first to use the involvement of the state in the reproduction process to reconcile theoretically the temporary stability of capitalism with the continued existence of its basic contradictions.[67] Although originally this was an extremely controversial argument, in the 1960s it was increasingly accepted and became the core of the 'stamocap' theories. Already today several systematic expositions of the theory exist.[68] In the Soviet Union an extensive 'Political Economy of Contemporary Monopoly Capitalism' has been produced by the Institute for World Economy and International Relations,[69] while there is also a similar systematic study by WYGODSKI;[70] in the new East German textbook of political economy the theory of state monopoly capitalism is accepted as the basis of current research.[71] In the GDR a team of economists have produced an analysis of the general economic structure of state monopoly capitalism,[72] while the work of the Institute for Social Sciences of the central committee of the SED has concentrated largely on political and historical aspects of the analysis of state monopoly capitalism in the FRG.[73] Outside of the socialist countries the most important contribution to the theory has been the discussion in France, out of which developed an extensive collective study commissioned by the PCF.[74] At a lower level of generality, there is now a growing number of empirical investigations on specific questions of state monopoly capitalism, together with an increasing number of studies of its historical development.

Despite the multitude of publications and a correspondingly broad range of opinions within them, the theory of state monopoly capitalism can be treated as a distinct theoretical current, since there are a number of theoretical points on which all its adherents agree.

1 State monopoly capitalism is treated as a specific phase of capitalist development within the historical sequence competitive capitalism – monopoly capitalism – state monopoly capitalism: state monopoly capitalism is seen as beginning at the end of the nineteenth century and being fully formed during the First World War. The theory therefore revives Lenin's concept of state monopoly capitalism in a way which claims both theoretical and historical continuity: it not only claims to continue Lenin's theory, but also treats the stage of state monopoly capitalism as being the same as that analysed by Lenin.

2 State monopoly capitalism means that the state regularly and systematically intervenes in economic affairs, so correcting and modifying economic laws. The theory holds that after a certain stage in capitalist development state intervention is an economic necessity if the growing valorization problems of capital are to be overcome. The advance of the

process of concentration and centralization of capital is taken as meaning that state intervention primarily benefits the monopolies, whose own economic power therefore expands in line with the expansion of the extra-economic power of the state.

3   State monopoly capitalism is treated as part of the 'general crisis of capitalism'. There are several aspects to this argument which vary in importance in the different versions of the theory. Firstly, state intervention acts to restrain temporarily such destabilizing consequences of the capitalist system as cyclical crises, even though it cannot overcome the discrepancy within capitalism between the ability to consume and the ability to produce. Secondly, this stabilizing effect of state intervention goes with (and also partially causes) the appearance of further destabilizing moments (e.g. inflation, currency crises, unemployment, sectoral crises). On balance therefore state intervention does not reduce the crisis-proneness of capitalism, but merely makes it manifest itself in latent instability instead of cyclical crises. Thirdly, just as in the earlier Comintern analyses, a central part of the 'general crisis' is the contraction of the area of capitalist rule as a result of decolonization and system competition.

4   The different versions of the theory of state monopoly capitalism all agree on the analysis's political consequences: since state monopoly capitalism means the extensive socialization of production, it therefore forms the material basis for socialism. This 'economic maturity' of capitalism however is no substitute for political action and the actual transition to socialism can only come about as a result of the 'anti-monopoly struggle'. In this struggle the working class seeks alliances with all other classes and strata (up to and including the self-employed middle class) which are detrimentally affected by state monopoly capitalism. This strategy is known in Germany as the 'broad anti-monopoly alliance'[75] and in France as 'revolutionary action for democracy and socialism.'[76]

This attempt to find a basic argument common to the different theories of state monopoly capitalism is not intended to create a homogeneity which does not exist in reality. Within the limits of these general assumptions the different theories often vary widely from each other. For example in the French analysis the necessity of the increasing state intervention in contemporary capitalism is deduced in theoretical terms from the tendency of the rate of profit to fall, overaccumulation and the problems of capital valorization.[77] By contrast, in the Soviet textbook of political economy the transition from monopoly capitalism to state monopoly capitalism is justified only in terms of description of the empirical forms of increased state activity – the increasing importance of the monopolies for the economy as a whole, the scientific-technical revolution, social welfare policy, system competition.[78] As these examples suggest, any adequate presentation of the current state of the discussion would have to compare point by point the different theories of state monopoly capitalism, and this is something which cannot be attempted here.

Since the theory of state monopoly capitalism is the official theory of the 'concretely existing socialism' in the Soviet Union and the other socialist countries, as well as the official theory of many communist parties in the capitalist countries, it has a prominent place within contemporary socialist political economy. However, as is well known, it is not universally accepted and indeed is heavily criticized by independent Marxists. Politically, the central question in the discussion is whether the strategy which follows from the theory really is a way towards a revolutionary transformation of society, or whether in fact it is far more a defensive ideology which allows the socialist states and the established communist parties to settle down comfortably to a longer period of system competition.[79] Theoretically, the basic issue is whether the theory of state monopoly capitalism is consistent with the basic assumptions of a Marxist political economy.[80]

At the present moment it can hardly yet be claimed that a systematic discussion and criticism exists, but nonetheless it is possible to sketch out the problems which are at issue. This can be done in terms of the four aspects of the different theories of state monopoly capitalism which have already been listed above.

1   The most problematic part of the theory is probably its historical reconstruction of the state monopoly capitalist state. The theory of state monopoly capitalism obscures such historical ruptures as the demobilization of 1918 and the new state intervention with economic stabilization policies after the world economic crisis of 1929/32, just as it obscures the differences between the functions of the state in contemporary capitalism and its functions for example in the First World War. Here clearly the theoretical and political appeal to Lenin is obviously an obstacle to the re-examination of both history and the history of theory.[81]

2   Like Lenin in his own period, the theory of state monopoly capitalism is certainly quite correct in drawing attention to the growing economic importance of the state. However, the theory of state monopoly capitalism is not a systematic theory of the state: the functioning of the state is not treated as an integral part of the economic analysis but instead as something purely exogenous to the economy. As a result, the theory does not provide any systematic account of what the possibilities and the limits of state intervention actually are, just as it leaves completely open how the activity of the state is determined by economic development. At best these questions are answered with *ad hoc* formulae. To take a concrete example, the monopolies' control over the state is not related to the political demand for an anti-capitalist democracy within the unaltered framework of the capitalist mode of production. The fact that the state can be placed outside the economic process in this fashion is obviously related to the basic methodological position of the theory of state monopoly capitalism: capitalism as a mode of production is seen as basically already historically redundant and only able to survive thanks to the extra-economic power of the state. In other words, the theory of state monopoly capitalism sees the state as something completely outside the economic

process. Critics of this position are quite justified in appealing to Marx here, because for Marx the functions of the state in general (and not just the concrete state of the nineteenth century) have to be integrally related to the process of the valorization of capital.

3   The most important theoretical break with Marx seems to be the new definition of the crisis, which follows Lenin's idea of the 'decay' of capitalism and the Comintern's formula of the 'general crisis'. The problem here is not that Marx's theory is modified (by itself something which is completely legitimate) but that in the theory of state monopoly capitalism manifestations of the crisis are only empirically described rather than, as previously, being deduced from the movement of capital itself. Consequently, the different publications based on the theory list different elements of the general crisis and only are able to relate these elements to each other in a very *ad hoc* fashion.

4   Finally the strategic consequences of the theory of state monopoly capitalism are also extremely problematic. The starting point of the programme of the anti-monopolist alliance is the claimed discrepancy between the objective class situation of the proletariat and its actual class consciousness. On the one hand contemporary capitalism is defined as redundant, on the other hand this 'redundant' capitalism is somehow able to create a completely false consciousness amongst the masses.[82] The original starting point of Marx's political economy is dissolved into, on the one side, a theory of economic functions, on the other side, the political demand for the transformation of the capitalist mode of production. The theory thus is completely lacking in any materialist analysis capable of linking class consciousness and political action.

5

RECENT DEVELOPMENTS IN MARXIST ECONOMIC THEORY

During the last few years, Marxism has flourished in many parts of the western world and particularly in universities. This presents problems in assessing recent developments in Marxist economic theory, partly because of the quantity of material to be surveyed, partly because of rapid developments and changes in theoretical emphasis, but also because of the commitment intrinsic to Marxism to relate theory to practical issues of struggle and not to separate economics out as an independent social science. These problems should be borne in mind whenever this chapter exposes rough edges in its critical appraisal of various contributions and whenever it imposes a rough justice of heavy precis to them. This chapter was prepared whilst the author was in the process of writing the book *Rereading Capital* with Laurence Harris. There the interested reader will find the issues covered here, and others, treated at greater length. This chapter, particularly its first two sections, is also more difficult than the earlier chapters since it covers the complex issues that have concerned recent debates. For reasons that will become clear, it presupposes a certain knowledge of orthodox economic theory. The reader having difficulty is advised to persist with the chapter and follow up the appropriate references given if necessary.

1. Value and the Transformation Problem

One issue that has focused differences between Marxist economists has been the so-called transformation problem. According to one school of thought,[1] dubbed neo-Ricardian, this problem involves an analysis of the relationship between values and prices. As is well known, an equalized rate of profit is incompatible with the exchange of commodities at their values, once the organic composition of capital differs between industries. Marx confronted this difficulty by arguing that surplus value was not distributed amongst capitalists according to the amount produced in individual factories, but according to the capital advanced in each factory. Surplus value in aggregate could be seen as a social pool, from which capitalists draw in proportion to the amount of capital used as opposed to their contribution to the pool.[2] Marx was mistaken, however, in measuring capital advanced in terms of values, whereas the results of his own analysis suggests that capital is advanced in money terms at prices of production that diverge from values. Commodities cannot sell at one price but be purchased at another.

Whilst Marx did recognize this discrepancy in his analysis, he proceeded regardless. For neo-Ricardians however, the discrepancy must not only be corrected but must also lead to a complete rejection of Marxist value theory *as they conceive it* (see below). They do not and cannot deny the possibility of amending Marx's transformation.[3] What they do argue is that a value theory based on labour-time is irrelevant, since the desired prices of production and rate of profit can be obtained without reference to values at all. This is done simply by determining the price of any commodity by marking up its cost of production (physical means of production multiplied by their prices plus labour times the wage) by the rate of profit. The result is a set of simultaneous equations from which prices and the rate of profit can be deduced once the level of wages is known.

Not surprisingly there has been a strong reaction against neo-Ricardianism because of its destructive implications for value theory, the very foundation of Marx's political economy. Typically, this reaction takes the form of defending Marx's theory against the variously perceived neo-Ricardian mis-interpretations of it. As such it has varying degrees of validity according to the extent that it represents Marx correctly *and* criticizes neo-Ricardianism rather than simply counterposing Marx to neo-Ricardianism. In these terms, the most common criticism[4] is the one that neo-Ricardianism interprets Marx's concept of value as simply being the socially necessary labour-time of production. As such Marx's concept of value is reduced to and identified with Ricardo's. In contrast, Marx's value theory, whilst based on labour-time, draws the distinction between the substance of value and its expression or form of existence in exchange as a price. It is a theory of the *form of value* focusing on the two-fold nature of the commodity (use-value and exchange value) in correspondence to the two-fold nature of labour (concrete and abstract) in a commodity-producing society.[5]

Another line of criticism of neo-Ricardianism is that they misinterpret the significance of the transformation problem. For them, it is simply a question of deriving prices and the profit rate from values (the latter becoming a redundant detour in the derivation of the former). In contrast, the relationship between value and its form can be re-examined on the basis of capitalist commodity production and its associated economic relations. Baumol interprets Marx as attempting to show how the production of surplus value is integrated as a social process with its distribution.[6] Gerstein interprets the transformation as an analysis of the integration of the production of value (and surplus value) with its circulation in exchange.[7] Fine and Harris argue that the transformation is to be seen as an analysis of how the production, distribution and exchange of (surplus) value is brought about.[8] In this perspective, based on the circuit of capital,[9] other approaches to the transformation can be assessed. In particular, neo-Ricardians can be seen to be preoccupied with relations of distribution and exchange at the expense of an integration of these with the process of producing value. In contrast, Marx did examine the relationships between the three economic processes, but failed to do so adequately, not transforming the value of capital as it is *redistributed* through *exchange* for the purposes of *production* (i.e. as means of production and labour-power are purchased by the capitalist as inputs). What Marx did do was to transform values as they emerge from *production* as commodities to be *exchanged* at a uniform rate of profit thereby *redistributing* surplus value.

Neo-Ricardians have also been criticized on what may be termed 'sociological' grounds. As they base their analysis on the confrontation of capital and labour in exchange and distribution (over the level of wages paid, for example, rather than over the coercion to create surplus value during the production process) neo-Ricardians fail to distinguish capitalism as a specific mode of production, one in which freedom of exchange conceals the confines of the class relations of production. Indeed, as Rowthorn observes, in the equations employed by neo-Ricardians, there is no reason to believe that it is capitalists that employ wage-labour rather than workers who hire machines.[10]

The debate, as it stands so far discussed, simply counterposes interpretations of Marx's theory with neo-Ricardianism. As such, it appears as if there is a choice of the one theory or the other, neo-Ricardianism does have the disadvantage of rejecting Marx's authority, but also the advantage of demonstrating the nonsense of those who regard Marx's transformation as sacrosanct and beyond reproach.[11] However, those who remain committed to value theory can do so because of its specific relation to capitalist commodity production. The significance of this has been brought out through an exchange between Hodgson (a neo-Ricardian) and Fine and Harris.[12] In response to Hodgson's question of why values are necessary for the analysis of capitalist production, Fine and Harris give three related reasons each linked to the method of Marxism. First, analysis of values is an immediate appropriation in thought of the determining contradiction in capitalism; the confrontation between capital and labour in production in abstraction from the mediation between the classes through distribution and exchange. (In contrast, neo-Ricardianism introduces competition between many capitals at the outset − to equalize the rate of profit − and competition between labourers − to equalize the level of wages). Second, the dynamic development of capitalist production − through accumulation, centralization and the introduction of machinery − depends fundamentally on the antagonisms between capital and labour in the production process (rather than technical change in response to price and wage changes as suggested by neo-Ricardianism). Third, the unity between production, distribution and exchange is a complex one and does not simply have the function in theory of revealing the sociology of capitalist exploitation. Rather, the tensions and displacements between these economic spheres of activity must be explored to understand the nature of the crises that punctuate periods of accumulation. This is to be done on the basis of revealing how the fundamental contradiction between capital and labour in production is reproduced in its relation to distribution and exchange.[13] (In contrast, neo-Ricardians base themselves on a concept of the economy which utilizes a simple unity of production, distribution and exchange, one in which each counts equally conceptually, rejecting value analysis since it becomes redundant on the basis of their price equations).

2. Sraffian Economics

So far we have discussed some recent contributions to an assessment of Marx's value theory. However, related to these debates has been the development of a criticism of neo-classical economics (the bourgeois orthodoxy[14]) based on the work of Sraffa and subsequently Robinson.[15] Essentially, criticism is of the neo-classical theory of distribution based on the marginal productivity of inputs and of capital in particular (that the marginal product of capital determines the rate of profit). The result of the neo-classical theory is that given knowledge of all possible techniques of production and of the particular one in use, it is possible to determine the rate of profit (and wages) in a competitive economy by the marginal product of capital (labour) since capitalists will set the two equal to maximize profitability. This result is shown to be false in general by the followers of Sraffa if the economy contains more than one commodity. It is demonstrated that there is an inverse relationship between the level of wages and the rate of profit. Competition merely ensures that at any given level of wages (rate of profit) the technique of production actually used will be the one that generates the corresponding highest rate of profit (level of wages). A particular technique may sustain the highest rate of profit for two or even more different levels of wages so that there is no unique correspondence between the particular technique in use and a particular distribution between capital and labour in the form of wages and profit. The marginal productivity theory becomes at best circular since the rate of profit is the ratio of surplus to capital advanced in money terms. To evaluate this ratio (in an economy with more than one good) and in particular the denominator, it is necessary to know relative prices. These in turn depend upon the rate of profit which cannot therefore be determined by the marginal product of capital since this can only be determined once the rate of profit is already known.[16]

Sraffian economics has attracted the attention of radical economists because of its supposedly destructive implications for the neo-classical theory of distribution. In addition, it has the attraction of posing an alternative theory of distribution based on class struggle over the level of wages and profits. For, as we have seen, the theory suggests, on the basis of given technology, that there is an irreducible conflict between capital and labour over the surplus product. However, the significance of Sraffian economics cannot itself be assessed by the extent to which it attracts radical economists but according to its scientific validity.

First, it must be pointed out that the Sraffian economics used as a criticism of neo-classical economics is essentially identical to the neo-Ricardian economics that is used to criticize Marxist value theory (as discussed in the previous section). As such, its validity in explaining distribution between capital and labour (and other phenomena) is subject to the same criticisms that are levelled against neo-Ricardianism as well as others that emerge as its status in criticizing neo-classical economics is assessed. On this score, the Sraffian critique is extremely limited and can be considered more a reconstruction of a (corrected) neo-classical economics on its own terms rather than a break with it.[17] This can be seen in a number of related ways.

To begin with the critique is only relevant for the one-good model of neo-classical economics, for which distribution is determined by the marginal product of capital alone. It shows that a world with more than one good cannot in general be reduced to behaviour as if it were only a one-good world – hardly a surprising result. This is done precisely by constructing the *neo-classical theory of production* for the many-good world (individual capitalists maximize profits on the basis of given prices, wages and technology). Where the critique departs from the *orthodox* neo-classical approach is in suggesting that the resulting inverse relation between the level of wages and the rate of profit is 'closed' by class struggle over distribution rather than by intertemporal preferences between present and future consumption (i.e. maximization of individual utility over time). It is precisely this neo-classical general equilibrium of production and consumption that the Sraffian critique leaves untouched, merely posing class distributional struggle as an alternative to the theory of consumption. In this light it is hardly surprising that the best representatives of neo-classical theory[18] embrace the Cambridge critique as correct and acceptable (after initial birth pangs), delighting in its potential for attacking Marxist value theory, whilst leaving the fundamentals of neo-classical theory untouched.

3. The Law of the Tendency of the Rate of Profit to Fall

Apart from value theory itself, debates among Marxist economists have also concerned the laws of motion of capitalism and in particular, the law of the tendency of the rate of profit to fall, TRPF. Before assessing the various contributions, it is necessary to supplement the interpretation of Marx's analysis outlined earlier.[19] First, Marx's law of the TRPF was a theory of the cycle of production and as a result had no implications as such for the long-term movements in the rate of profit. However, the cycle of production is not a neutral concept but has a different meaning for each economist. For Marx, it was fundamentally a cycle of accumulation with which was to be associated a *restructuring* of capital. Accumulation is not a balanced, proportionate expansion, but one that requires centralization through acquisition, merger and bankruptcy. This is a process resulting not only in fierce competition between capitalists, but also between classes as the reorganization and intensive extension of capitalist production enlarges and strengthens the proletariat whilst simultaneously subjecting it to revolutionary changes in economic and social conditions. Second, Marx's consideration of the law and the counteracting tendencies is undertaken at a high level of abstraction. The categories utilized do not correspond to the immediate complex phenomena of the concrete world which can only be constructed at a subsequent stage of analysis. Third, related to this, the law is not an empirical prediction, either for cyclical or secular movements of the rate of profit, but is a working out of the forces underlying these movements rather than a resolution of them.

These considerations are made clear by the structure of Marx's argument, most notably by the titles of the three chapters in Volume III of *Capital* that he devotes to the law, *The Law as Such*, *The Counteracting Influences* and *The Internal Contradictions of the Law*. In this last chapter, it is the conflict between the law and the counteracting tendencies that is the subject of analysis. But this is not treated as a simple addition of the positive and negative effects on the rate of profit, rather as an analysis of the outcome of the simultaneous operation of the two sets of tendencies, almost irrespective of what happens to the resulting rate of profit. For 'crises are always but momentary and forcible solutions of the existing (internal) contradictions.'[20]

Now recent interpretations of the law of the TRPF have been dominated by two schools. The first neo-Ricardian interpretation rejects the law on empirical and theoretical grounds,[21] because the organic composition of capital has not risen and because there is no reason why the law of the TRPF should dominate the counteracting tendencies even if it had. Consequently this misinterpretation of the law suffers from seeing it as making immediate empirical predictions and embodies an understanding of the interaction between the TRPF and the counteracting tendencies as a simple sum of the two effects. In addition, it is developed to explain actual falls in the rate of profit simply by the growth of wages as a result of working-class distributional struggle.

The second interpretation of the law is the one that insists on its validity[22] by reworking Marx's analysis of the rising organic composition but continues by asserting the dominance of the tendency over the counteracting tendencies rather than theorizing the contradictory interaction of the two. In this light, such a view can be considered to be an extreme version of the neo-Ricardian analysis in which distributional struggle, increases in the rate of exploitation and decreases in the value of capital are considered dogmatically to be of secondary significance relative to the TRPF. Thus, the simple interaction of the two tendencies as a sum must lead to an actual fall in the rate of profit.

These two apparently opposing interpretations of the law then have much in common and consequently have stunted rather than developed Marxist theory. Because both view the law of the TRPF as resulting in empirical falls in the rate of profit, and have associated falls in the rate of profit (whatever the cause) with crises, it has not been considered necessary to elaborate the 'internal contradictions' between the two tendencies to arrive at a theory of crisis that integrates the process of capitalist accumulation and production of surplus value with its distribution and exchange.

4. The Current Recession

The development of Marxist economics in recent years has not simply revolved around pure issues of theory, as surveyed above, but has been concerned with the relevance of that theory to developments in the world economy. In particular, it has been necessary to explain the current world economic recession in the light of the 'post-war boom.' In this, attention has focused on a number of different issues – the general nature of the crisis, the role played by state economic intervention, the changing nature of imperialism – and each is generally recognized as being related to the others. Nevertheless, it remains the case that no successful integration and explanation of these phenomena has been accomplished. Indeed, analyses have often proceeded, as we shall see, as if oblivious to their inconsistencies with developments that are not their immediate object of study.

To begin with explanations of the crisis, theorists have simply applied their ideas to their conception of the particular conditions prevailing in the world economy. As a result, explanations have more or less inevitably fallen prey in one form or another to Keynesian notions infused with a Marxist rhetoric. This is most clear in the case of under-consumptionist theories, originating in modern times with the work of Baran and Sweezy.[23] Here it is argued that there is in the era of monopoly capitalism an inevitable tendency for capitalism to be unable to sell the goods that it can produce. On the other hand, the monopolization of industry enables firms to raise prices and increase profits without fear of competition unduly reducing sales. Simultaneously, banks and other institutions *over*-expand credit to maintain what deficient demand and output they can but necessarily produce inflation.[24] Unfortunately, the separate elements of the theory simply cannot fit together. A false dichotomy is drawn between monopoly and competition (as in orthodox economics) whilst stagflation is explained by the simultaneous existence of excess and deficient demand (what constitutes the crisis of Keynesian theory).

Whilst underconsumptionists tend to place relatively little emphasis on distributional struggle (except to observe that low wages implies low demand for wage goods), this is the centrepiece of neo-Ricardian analysis. Denying the law of the tendency of the rate of profit to fall, they nevertheless argue that falling profitability is brought about by the increasingly successful struggle by workers for wage increases. For Glyn and Sutcliffe, the intensification of competition internationally is another blade in the scissors of the 'profit squeeze.'[25] Within this framework, inflation can be explained as a product of and weapon in distributional struggle between capital and labour as in orthodox theories of wage-push.

Those that argue the validity of the law of the TRPF by asserting the dominance of the tendency over the counteracting tendencies view the current recession in terms of the particular response by capital to the inevitable working of the law. In particular, the state is seen as being compelled to expand expenditure to maintain employment for political stability. The result of this is a further diminution in the surplus value available for distribution to capitalists as profits, and inflation as the state expands its credit to finance its expenditure. Inevitably, the crisis is only postponed by these manoeuvres. Again, we can see that a Keynesian analysis has been adopted (together with a Keynesian view of the role of the state to maintain employment) with the (false) presumption that state expenditure will increase employment even though profitability has been affected. In addition, a monetarist theory of inflation has been utilized with the (false) presumption that the state predominantly appropriates resources through over-expansion of the money supply.[26]

Other theorists, most notably Mandel and Rowthorn, tend to adopt all of these explanations simultaneously, rejecting mono-causal theories of the current recession.[27] Shortage of labour, increasing organic composition of capital, and distributional struggle are all seen as factors contributing to the formation of the rate of profit and the pace of accumulation. Such analyses are all-embracing at the expense of being eclectic and are also unsystematic theoretically, necessarily drawing arbitrarily upon the 'significant' factors. Fine and Harris have, however, rejected such an approach by interpreting the current recession in terms of the cycle of restructuring of production associated with the law of TRPF.[28] They argue that the state does not and cannot abolish crises (as Keynesians argue) nor that it is committed (unsuccessfully) to full employment, but that it intervenes in and promotes the cycle, tempering its rhythm (so at times it precipitates and prolongs recessions). Fundamental to this is the restructuring of capital from which struggles over distribution and employment are related but derivative. Consequently, state economic intervention should be seen primarily in relation to its effects on the restructuring of capital (most clearly for nationalizations and aid to private industry) even where this is not the direct object of intervention (as for incomes policy etc.). The problem of this approach is its tendency to reduce everything to the logic of restructuring, but this is necessarily so only as long as the complex relationships between the restructuring of capital and derivative phenomena are untheorized. As we have argued, this is a task that cannot be avoided if Marxist analysis of the economy is to free itself from dependency upon Keynesianism.

In our survey of contributions in this section we have necessarily touched upon the role played by state economic intervention. This is in turn an issue of debate that has been stimulated from two different directions (but which we can only mention briefly in passing). First, as we have seen, there has been consideration of the relationship between the state and the economic laws of motion of capitalism. For neo-Ricardians in particular, but also for others from time to time who adopt a Keynesian framework, the state intervenes to deflate the economy when wage pressures through high employment threaten the rate of profit. In addition, the state makes economic interventions to moderate class struggle (by granting social welfare) and organize capital efficiently as far as possible and hence raise profitability[29] (by providing infrastructure etc.) Such an analysis has been criticized not only for its rejection of capital's laws of motion but also for its rejection of Marx's categories of political economy.[30] For whether economic activity is organized by capital or not (whether privately or by the state) is irrelevant, for what counts is only its supposed contribution to the rate of profit. All economic activities are reduced to a common denominator and for this reason the significance of the distinction between productive and unproductive labour is also essentially rejected. In contrast, it can be argued that the state must respond to the results of the law of the TRPF (see above) or more correctly that the state is increasingly integrated into the complex operation of the law.[31]

The second approach to the problem of the role of state economic intervention has been to explore the relationship between politics and economics in the capitalist mode of production. Stimulated (often to criticism) by the work of Althusser and Balibar and Poulantzas,[32] consideration has been given to the general nature of the *capitalist* state, that is how it is based on the existence of capitalist relations of production and their development rather than on the necessity of performing general functions in a capitalist society (such as law and order etc.). In this light, the role of state economic intervention is not seen in terms of political response to economic developments, but as the articulated development of political and economic relations.[33]

5. Imperialism and the World Economy

There is little doubt that Lenin's *Imperialism* has had a dominating influence on Marxist analyses of the world economy. The changing conditions generated by a further sixty years of capital accumulation on a world scale have left untouched the view that blocs of capital are organized in conjunction with readily identifiable nation-states each of which serves the function of pursuing the economic interests of its bloc of capital in rivalry with others. It is recognized that the forms and balance of conflict may have changed, but otherwise the organizing principles of analysis are undisturbed.

That this is an unsatisfactory state of theoretical affairs can be seen in the light of all-embracing analyses of developments in the world economy. In this context, the most significant work concerns the internationalization of capital, not only for exports and finance as emphasized by Lenin, but also for capital in production itself. Increasingly, through multi-national corporations, production is organized (and reorganized over the cycle) across national boundaries.[34] Clearly such a development cannot be mapped out without bringing into question the theoretical framework that places a bloc of capital under the umbrella of a single nation-state. Nevertheless imprisoned within this framework, some writers[35] have posed the internationalization of capital as a development to be assessed in terms of the strength of the nation-state versus that of the multi-national corporation. Murray argues that the choice of nation for location of production open to the corporation weakens the power of the nation chosen because of the alternatives available, whereas Warren argues that monopolization and increasing state economic intervention strengthen the nation-state's control in its relations with individual corporations. Whatever the theoretical deficiencies of these two approaches in other respects, each presumes that there is a conflict between nation-states and internationalizing capital, whereas the proper starting point should be the role played by state economic intervention to promote internationalization.

In this light, state economic intervention cannot be taken as a simple indicator of the pursuit of the interests of a nation's capital. When this is done the almost inevitable result is an analysis that parallels Keynesianism.[36] Overexpansion of domestic credit to maintain production leads to inflation, lack of international competitiveness and pressure for exchange rate devaluation. Consequently, inter-imperialist rivalries are located in terms of the economic and political state policies adopted to gain international advantage in the face of these constraints. The internationalization of (productive) capital fades into the background and is forgotten as the analysis is forced into the rigid framework of capitals competing internationally through determinate nation-states.[37]

Related to much of this work is an assessment of how the balance of power between nation-states has changed and is changing. At one level, it involves a whole series of indices of strength, each embodying an arbitrary element and rarely being rooted in any theoretical structure. Whether the particular index chosen is export performance (or import penetration), domestic productivity increase (or profitability), the international strength of national currency, or the foreign ownership of assets, none can be satisfactory since a complex category superficially analysed cannot serve as substitute for a structured analysis (even if the underlying model of inter-imperialist rivalry could be accepted despite the increasingly nation-less character of internationalizing capital). At another level, the assessment of the balance of power between nation-states is seen in terms of a reordering of alliances. For Mandel, in particular, a European formation is the logical response to American (and Japanese) hegemony and he draws the crudely mechanical need for an European state to correspond to a European economy.[38]

An alternative to the approaches already discussed is offered by Poulantzas.[39] He puts aside theories that rely upon a concept of the power of the state as such but instead sees it as expressing and crystallizing class powers. In the context of internationalization, this involves groups of the bourgeoisie including internal and international fractions. Poulantzas also correctly sees the internationalization of capital in production as a driving force of the current world economy, but he incorrectly subordinates all other forces to it. Constructing a chain of imperialism headed by the USA, he neglects the role played by state economic intervention in defiance of the international bourgeoisie (whether in response to national fractions or proletariat) and paradoxically also the role of international state apparatuses (such as the EEC, IMF etc). In short, the current period of imperialism, driven by cooperation and rivalry through the internationalization of capital and state economic intervention, gives rise to increasingly complex phenomena. There are no shortcuts to an understanding of these phenomena, for these would, as we have seen, necessarily by-pass the underlying forces which give rise to the phenomena concerned. Just as for an analysis of crises, we have found that Marxists too readily abandon abstract categories, either altogether or prematurely, in the leap to confront the complexity of concrete reality.

So far we have failed to discuss imperialism and the world economy in terms of advanced and underdeveloped countries, of relations between metropolis and periphery. One school of thought has dominated this arena, that associated with unequal exchange. That it has proved so popular, however, does not reflect its scientific validity as much as its ready correspondence with an anti-imperialist ideology. For it is argued that the world capitalist market allows nations of the periphery to be exploited by those of the metropolis even where rates of profit are equalized internationally. In the work of Frank, this is accomplished through the transfer of value from economies with low levels of development to the more developed, and, for Emmanuel, through lower levels of wages in the periphery than in the metropolis.[40]

These theories have, however, been subject to a mounting tide of criticism, focusing on a number of related issues. First, unequal exchange is an exchange based theory of exploitation of one nation by another rather than a production based theory of exploitation of one class by another.[41] Second, countries at different stages of capitalist development and even pre-capitalist organizations are essentially treated identically simply because they produce commodities exchanged on the world market, thus subordinating their own internal laws of development to the distributive coercion of external capital.[42] Third, unequal exchange can only theorize uneven development after the fact and as a result of coercion by imperialist powers to appropriate surplus labour. It is not explained why greater surplus (whether exchanged equally or not) could not be appropriated through the coerced development of the periphery.[43]

What these criticisms bring to light is the need to develop a theory of underdevelopment that confronts the role played by imperialist capital in promoting or hindering the development of the class relations of production in the periphery. Far from this being a simple economic theory, it will involve an understanding of the laws of motion of pre-capitalist as well as of capitalist modes of production. In addition, the articulation of metropolis and periphery necessarily presupposes an examination of the class alliances formed within dependent nations through the state and how these express the interests of an indigenous ruling class and an external fraction of internationalizing capital.[44] In short, just as in our earlier considerations, there can be no simple leap from general theoretical abstractions (even when these are correct) to an understanding of complex and concrete developments.

Notes

Chapter I

1 The most important advocates of cooperative ideas were Robert Owen in England and Charles Fourier in France.

2 Cf. C. Grünberg, 'Der Ursprung der Worte "Sozialismus" und "Sozialist"', *Archiv für die Geschichte des Sozialismus und der Arbeiterbewegung* (edited by C. Grünberg) 2 (1912), 372ff.

3 F. Engels, *Anti-Dühring* (London, 1955), 365.

4 Cf. A. Menger, *Das Recht auf den vollen Arbeitsertrag* (Stuttgart, 1886).

5 For this section of Ch. I compare the discussions in: W. Hofmann, *Ideengeschichte der sozialen Bewegung des 19. und 20. Jahrhunderts* (Berlin 1970); M. Beer, *Allgemeine Geschichte des Sozialismus und der sozialen Kämpfe* (Berlin, 1931; reprinted 1971); T. Ramm, *Die grossen Sozialisten als Rechts- und Sozialphilosophen*, vol. 1 (Stuttgart, 1955); G. Cole, *A History of Socialist Thought: vol. 1, The Forerunners 1789–1850* (London, 1962); L.-v.Stein, *Geschichte der sozialen Bewegung in Frankreich von 1789 bis auf unsere Tage*, vols. 2 & 3 (1850; reprinted Darmstadt, 1972).

6 Cf. the texts reprinted in M. Vester (ed.), *Die Frühsozialisten 1789–1848*, vol. 1 (Reinbek, 1970), 151ff; T. Ramm (ed.), *Der Frühsozialismus*, Quellentexte (Stuttgart, 1968) 6ff. The classic account of the life and teachings of Babeuf is P. Buonarrotti, *Buonarrotti's History of Babeuf's Conspiracy for Equality* (1836).

7 T. Spence, *The Nationalization of Land* (1775).

8 Cf. T. Spence, *The Restoration of Society to its Natural State* (1801); idem, *The End of Oppression* (1795).

9 Cf. Spence, *The Nationalization* ...

10 C. Hall, *The Effects of Civilization* (1805).

11 Cf. T. Paine, *The Rights of Man* (1791/1792); idem, Agrarian Justice (1797).

12 Cf. Hall, *op. cit.*

13 Cf. the reprint of the correspondence in O. Rudkin, *Thomas Spence and his Connections* (New York, 1966), 130ff.

14 Cf. H. de Saint-Simon, 'L'Organisateur', in *Oeuvres de Claude-Henri de Saint-Simon*, Publiées par les membres du Conseil institué par Enfantin, vol. 3 (1869, reprinted Paris, 1966); idem, 'Du systeme industriel (1821–22)', in *Oeuvres ...*, vols. 5–7. Cf. also R. Fehlbaum, *Saint-Simon und die Saint-Simonisten. Vom Laissez-Faire zur Wirtschaftsplanung* (Basle and Tübingen, 1970).

15 Cf. M. Hahn, *Präsozialismus: Claude-Henri de Saint-Simon* (Stuttgart, 1970), 54ff.

16 According to Saint-Simon the 'industrialists' (les industriels) made up ⁴⁄₅ of the population. Cf. Saint-Simon, 'Catéchisme des Industriels', in *Oeuvres ...*, vol. 8, 13.

17 The achievement principle was later given a striking formulation by the Saint-Simonists with their slogan: *à chacun selon sa capacité, à chaque capacité selon ses oeuvres* [on the achievement principle cf. C. Offe, *Industry and Inequality* (London, 1976), esp. 41.].

18 Saint-Simon stressed what he saw as the praiseworthy good relationship of the French proletarians to their employers and accused the English workers of hostility towards capitalists, cf. H. de Saint-Simon, 'Über die Gesellschaftsorganisation,' in T. Ramm, (ed.), *Der Frühsozialismus*, 96.

19 Thus, according to Saint-Simon, the old system had been governed by men directly, whereas in the new society the action of men would be determined by principles. Cf. *idem*, 'L'Organisateur,' in *Oeuvres ...*, vol. 4, 197.

20 Cf. H. de Saint-Simon, 'Über die Gesellschaftsorganisation,' 98.

21 The most famous were Saint Armand Bazard (1791–1832) and Barthélémy-Prosper Enfantin (1796–1864).

22 Cf. the discussion of Saint-Simon's teachings in T. Ramm (ed.), *Der Frühsozialismus*, 130ff; P. Enfantin, *Oeuvres de Saint-Simon et d'Enfantin* (1868–76).

23 Cf. C. Fourier, *Théorie des quatres mouvements et des destinées générales* (Paris, 1808).

24 C. Fourier, *Théorie de l'Unité universelle*, vol. 4, in *Oeuvres complètes de Ch. Fourier*, vol. 5 (Paris, 1841; reprinted 1966), 486ff.

25 Cf. 'Ein Fragment Fouriers über den Handel' in T. Ramm (ed.), *Der Frühsozialismus*, 188ff; Wilhelm Weitling (1808–1871) supported this position, even though in other ways he rejected the theory that the three factors of capital, labour and talent all had to be rewarded; Weitling supported the abolition of private ownership in the means of production and called for a communist society based on the theory of value. Cf. W. Weitling, *Garantien der Harmonie und Freiheit* (1842; republished, with an introduction and notes by B. Kaufhold, Berlin, 1955), 43ff, 165ff, 233ff, 245f.

26 Cf. also C. Fourier, *Le nouveau monde industriel et sociétaire*, in *Oeuvres ...*, vol. 6, 99ff.

27 Cf. V. Considérant, *Exposition abrégée du système phalanstérien de Fourier* (Paris, 1845).

28 Cf. C. Fourier, *Théorie des quatres mouvements ...*

29 Cf. L. Blanc, *Organisation du Travail* (Paris, 1840). Cf. also the quotations from the book in M. Vester, *Die Frühsozialisten ...*, vol. 1, 210ff, also 'Zwei Reden im Luxembourg' in T. Ramm (ed.), *Der Frühsozialismus*, 446ff.

30 R. Owen, *A New View of Society* (1813–1814).

31 *Ibid.*

32 Cf. R. Owen, *Observations on the Effect of the Manufacturing System* (1815).

33 Cf. R. Owen, *Report to the County of Lanark* (1821).

34 Cf. R. Owen, 'Report to the Committee for the Relief of the Manufacturing Poor', in R. Owen, *A New View of Society and Other Essays*, introduced by G.D.H. Cole (London, 1966), 156ff. Owen's cooperative plans were probably one stimulus for the proposals for mitigating poverty put forward by the German Ludwig Gall (1790–1863). Cf. L. Gall, 'Mein Wollen und mein Wirken' (1835), in M. Vester, *Die Frühsozialisten 1789–1848*, vol. 2 (Reinbek, 1971), 44ff.

35 Cf. R. Owen, *Report ...*

36 *Ibid.*

37 For criticism of the theory of labour money cf. K. Marx, *Contribution to a Critique of Political Economy* (London, 1971), 83ff.

38 Cf. also Fourier's criticism of Owen's plans: C. Fourier, *Le Nouveau Monde ...*, 472ff.

39 Cf. W. Thompson, *An Enquiry into the Principles of the Distribution of Wealth most Conducive to Human Happiness* (1824).

40 Cf. W. Thompson, *Practical Directions for the Speedy and Economical Establishment of Communities* (1830); idem, *Appeal of one half the Human Race, Women, against the Pretentions of the other Half, Men, to Retain them in Political, and thence in Civil and Domestic, Slavery* (1825).
41 Cf. J. Gray, *A Lecture on Human Happiness* (1825); idem, *The Social System* (1831); idem, *An Efficient Remedy to the Distress of Nations* (1842).
42 Cf. J. Bray, *Labour's Wrongs and Labour's Remedy* (1839).
43 Cf. J. Morgan, *The Revolt of the Bees* (1826); idem, *The Christian Commonwealth* (1845).
44 Cf. T. Hodgskin, *Labour Defended Against the Claims of Capital* (1825); P.J. Proudhon, *Système des contradictions économiques, ou philosophie de la misère* (1846).
45 T. Hodgskin, *The Natural and Artificial Right of Property Contrasted* (1832), 48ff, 156ff. P. Proudhon, *Qu'est-ce que la propriété?* (1840).
46 W. Godwin, *An Enquiry Concerning Political Justice and its Influence on General Virtue and Happiness* (1793).
47 Cf. P. Ravenstone, *A Few Doubts on the Subject of Population and Political Economy* (London, 1821; new edition London, 1966), 208ff, 292ff; T. Hodgskin, *Popular Political Economy* (London, 1827), 20ff, 52.
48 Cf. P. Ravenstone, *A Few Doubts* ..., 25ff; T. Hodgskin, *The Natural and Artificial Right* ..., 173.
49 Cf. W. Thompson, *Labour Rewarded* (London, 1827).
50 P. Proudhon, *Le droit au travail et le droit de propriété* (1848); idem, *Système* ...
51 Cf. Proudhon, *Qu'est-ce que la propriété?*
52 Cf. P. Proudhon, *Organisation du crédit et de la circulation et solution du problème social* (1848).

Chapter 2

1 Cf. H. Grossmann, *Marx, Die klassische Nationalökonomie und das Problem der Dynamik* (1941) (Frankfurt/Vienna, 1969); H. Peter, 'Dynamische Theorie bei Marx und Keynes', *Jahrbuch für Nationalökonomie und Statistik* 162 (1950).
2 K. Marx and F. Engels, *The Communist Manifesto*, MESW, vol. 1, 137; as early as the Introduction to his *Critique of Hegel's Philosophy of Law*, Marx states that 'The *head* of this emancipation is philosophy, its heart is the *proletariat*', MECW, vol. 3, 187.
3 Cf. K. Marx, *A Contribution to the Critique of Political Economy* (London, 1971), 60; Marx to V. Annenkov, 28.12.1846, in K. Marx, F. Engels, V. Lenin, *On Historical Materialism* (Moscow, 1972), 273f. Cf. also A. Schmidt, 'Über Geschichte und Geschichtsschreibung in der materialistischen Dialektik', in *Folgen einer Theorie. Essays über 'Das Kapital' von Karl Marx* (Frankfurt, 1967), 103ff.
4 As is also explicitly argued in F. Engels, *Anti-Dühring* (London, 1955), 204.
5 Cf. Marx, 'Introduction' to *Contribution* ..., 210ff.
6 Cf. Marx, 'Introduction' to *Contribution* ..., 20f.
7 Cf. J. Zelený, *Die Wissenschaftslogik und 'Das Kapital'* (Frankfurt/Vienna, 1969); K. Korsch, *Karl Marx* (New York, 1963); A. Reichelt, *Zur logischen Struktur des Kapitalbegriffs bei Karl Marx* (Frankfurt/Vienna, 1972); O. Morf, *Geschichte und Dialektik in der politischen Ökonomie* (Frankfurt/Vienna, 1970): J. Schlelfstein, *Einführung in das Studium von Marx, Engels und Lenin* (Munich, 1972), 63ff.
8 Marx, *Contribution* ..., 20f; cf. also K. Marx & F. Engels, *The German Ideology*, MESW, vol. 1, 19ff.
9 Marx, *Contribution* ..., 20.
10 Cf. Marx, *Contribution* ..., 205ff.
11 Cf. also E. Iljenkow, 'Die Dialektik des Abstrakten und Konkreten im "Kapital" von Marx', in A. Schmidt (ed.), *Beiträge zur marxistischen Erkenntnistheorie*, (Frankfurt, 1970), 87ff.

84   *History of Socialist Economic Thought*

12 Cf. R. Rosdolsky, *Zur Entstehungsgeschichte des Marxschen 'Kapitals'*, vol. 1 (Frankfurt/Vienna, 1969), 24ff; H. Grossmann, 'Die Änderungen des ursprünglichen Aufbauplanes des Marxschen 'Kapitals' und ihre Ursachen', *Archiv für die Geschichte des Sozialismus und der Arbeiterbewegung* (Grünbergs Archiv) 14 (1929), 305ff; D. Rjazanov, 'Siebzig Jahre "Zur Kritik der Politischen Okonomie" ', *Archiv ...*, 15 (1930), 1ff.

13 The following sections two and three of this chapter follow closely the corresponding chapters of *Capital*, vol. 1. Cf. also P. Sweezy, *The Theory of Capitalist Development: Principles of Marxian Economy* (London, 1946); W. Hofmann, *Ideengeschichte der sozialen Bewegung des 19. und 20. Jahrhunderts* (Berlin, 1970), 101ff; L. Kühne, *Okonomie und Marxismus* (Neuwied and Berlin, 1972); J. Schleifstein, *op. cit.*, 95ff; R. Rosdolsky, *op. cit.*

14 Cf. Marx, *Contribution ...*, 28.

15 Cf. Marx, *Capital*, vol. 1, 36 (126); *idem, Contribution ...*, 28ff; *idem, Grundrisse* (London, 1973), 881; *idem, Wages, Prices and Profit*, MESW, vol. 2, 48ff; *idem, Randglossen zu Adolph Wagners 'Lehrbuch der politischen Ökonomie'*, MEW, vol. 19 (Berlin, 1972), 357ff. On the labour theory of value, cf. J. Rubin, *Studien zur Marxschen Werttheorie* (Frankfurt, 1973); M. Dobb, *Political Economy and Capitalism* (London, 1960), ch. 1–3; R. Meek, *Studies in the Labour Theory of Value* (London, 1956), 121ff; F. Petry, *Der soziale Gehalt der Marxschen Werttheorie* (Jena, 1916); J. Robinson, *Collected Economic Papers*, vol. 1 (Oxford, 1966), 146ff; vol. 2 (Oxford, 1964), 49ff; vol. 3 (Oxford, 1965), 173ff.

16 On the historical development of money, cf. Marx, *Grundrisse*, 165ff; *idem, Contribution ...*, 49ff. On the charaacteristics of money as (1) measure of value, (2) means of exchange, (3) material representation of wealth, cf. Marx, *Grundrisse*, 186ff; *idem, Capital*, vol. 1, 94ff; *idem, Contribution ...*, 64ff. Cf. also H. Backhaus, 'Zur Dialektik der Wertform', in A. Schmidt (ed.), *op. cit.* 128ff; B. Fritsch, *Die Geld- und Kredittheorie von Karl Marx* (Frankfurt and Vienna, 1968).

17 Marx, *Contribution ...*, 34.

18 Marx, *Capital*, vol. 1, 72 (164f).

19 On the problem of alienation which is touched on here, cf. K. Marx, *Economic and Philosophical Manuscripts of 1844*, MECW, vol. 3, 270ff; also Georg Lukacs, *History and Class Consciousness* (London, 1971), 83ff.

20 Cf. Marx, *Grundrisse*, 156f.

21 Marx, *Capital*, vol. 1, 92 (187).

22 *Ibid*, 80 (173).

23 *Ibid*, 148 (249).

24 *Ibid*, 150 (251f).

25 Cf. *ibid*, 156ff (258ff). In the circulation sphere no value is basically added to commodities, with the exception of transport labour, which strictly speaking is part of the production process. Cf. Marx, *Grundrisse*, 521ff, 533ff; *idem, Capital*, vol. 2, 129ff, 149ff.

26 Marx, *Capital*, vol. 1, 167 (270).

27 *Ibid*, 171 (274). Cf. also *idem, Grundrisse*, 266; *idem, Wage Labour and Capital*, MESW, vol. 1, 151ff; *idem, Wages, Prices and Profit*, MESW, vol. 2, 35ff; *idem, Results of the Immediate Process of Production*.

28 Cf. Marx, *Grundrisse*, 281ff.

29 In the form of surplus value. Cf. *Grundrisse*, 321ff.

30 Cf. Marx, *Capital*, vol. 1, 209 (317).

31 *Op. cit.*, 209 (317); *idem, Capital*, vol. 2, 157ff.

32 Cf. Marx, *Capital*, vol.1, 315 (432); *idem, Grundrisse*, 767ff; *idem, Results ...*, 1019ff.

33 Marx, *Capital*, vol. 1, 578 (724). Cf. also *idem, Grundrisse*, 690ff; *idem, Results ...*, 1060ff.

34 Marx, *Capital*, vol. 1, 592(739).
35 Cf. Marx, *Grundrisse* , 333ff, 386ff, 398ff; *idem*, *Capital*, vol. 3, 77ff.
36 Cf. Marx, *Capital*, vol. 1, 612(762).
37 Cf. Marx, *Capital*, vol. 1, 618(769).
38 *Ibid*, 619(880).
39 *Ibid*, 625(776f).
40 Cf. also Marx, *Capital*, vol. 3, 427ff.
41 Cf. Marx, *Capital*, vol. 1, 628ff(781ff).
42 *Ibid*, 632f(785).
43 Cf. Marx, *Grundrisse*, 604ff.
44 Marx, *Capital*, vol. 1, 645 (799). Cf. W. Hofmann, 'Verelendung', in *Folgen einer Theorie ...*, 27ff.
45 Marx, *Capital*, vol. 1, 763(929). Cf. also *idem*, *Grundrisse*, 749f.
46 Marx, *Capital*, vol. 3, 26ff.
47 Cf. the overview in L. von Bortkiewicz, 'Wertrechnung und Preisrechnung im Marxschen System', *Archiv für Sozialwissenschaft und Sozialpolitik* 23 (1906), 1ff; also *idem*, 'On the Correction of Marx's Fundamental Theoretical Construction in the Third Volume of Capital' (trans. Sweezy) in P. Sweezy (ed.), *Karl Marx and the Close of his System* (London, 1975). This volume also contains the classical contributions by Böhm-Bawerk ('Karl Marx and the Close of his System') and Hilferding ('Böhm-Bawerk's Criticism of Marx'). Cf. also F. Eberle (ed.), *Aspekte der Marxschen Theorie I. Zur methodischen Bedeutung des 3. Bandes des 'Kapital'* (Frankfurt, 1973).
48 Cf. especially Marx, *Capital*, vol. 3, 41ff.
49 Cf. *ibid*, 25ff, 49ff, 140ff, 152ff, 170ff.
50 Cf. Marx, *Theories of Surplus Value*, vol. 2, 27ff, *idem*, *Grundrisse*, 137.
51 Cf. Marx, *Capital*, vol. 3, 152ff. Marx's numerical examples were corrected and refined by Bortkiewicz, without challenging Marx's central assumptions. On this transformation problem and the explanatory claims of value thoery there is now an extensive literature and only a few titles are listed here: L. v. Bortkiewicz, 'Wertrechnung und Preisrechnung', *Archiv für Sozialwissenschaft und Sozialpolitik* 25 (1907), 10ff, 445ff; P. Sweezy, *Theory ...*, 109; K. Kühne, *op. cit.*, 154ff; P. Samuelson, 'Understanding the Marxian Notion of Exploitation', *Journal of Economic Literature* 9 (1971). Cf. also the contributions in F. Eberle, *Aspekte ...*, Parts 2 & 3.
52 Marx, *Capital*, vol. 1, 612(762); cf. *idem*, *Capital*, vol. 3, 143ff.
53 Cf. Marx, *Capital*, vol. 3, 207ff.
54 *Ibid*, 212; cf. also *idem*, *Grundrisse*, 764.
55 Marx, *Capital*, vol. 3, 229.
56 Cf. *ibid*, 230f, 84ff, 109ff, 244f.
57 Devaluation or destruction of capital also occurs especially in cyclically recurring crises. Cf. Marx, *Grundrisse*, 443ff; *idem*, *Theories of Surplus Value*, vol. 2, 495ff. In this way the contradictions which have become accentuated through the working of the tendency of the rate of profit to fall are temporarily checked and better valorization conditions are re-established. Cf. Marx, *Grundrisse*, 749f; *idem*, *Capital*, vol. 3, 245ff.
58 Cf. Marx, *Capital*, vol. 3, 230ff.
59 *Ibid*, 233.
60 J. Gillman, *Das Gesetz des tendenziellen Falls der Profitrate* (Frankfurt and Vienna, 1969); cf. also C. Rolshausen (ed.), *Kapitalismus und Krise* (Frankfurt and Vienna, 1970).
61 Cf. Sweezy, *Theory ...*, 102ff; Hofmann, *Ideengeschichte*, 140f.
62 Marx, *Capital*, vol. 3, 244, also 239f.
63 Cf. Marx, *Grundrisse*, 410ff.
64 Cf. Marx, *Theories of Surplus Value*, vol. 2, 497.
65 Marx, *Capital*, vol. 3, 472f.

66 Marx, *Capital*, vol. 2, 410f.
67 Marx, *Theories of Surplus Value*, vol. 2, 512.
68 Marx, *Capital*, vol. 3, 245.
69 Marx, *Theories of Surplus Value*, vol. 2, 492.
70 Marx, *Capital*, vol. 3, 253; cf. also *ibid*, 245ff. Further, Sweezy, *Theory ...*, 133ff; E. Preiser, 'Das Wesen der Marxschen Krisentheorie' (1924) in *idem*, *Politische Ökonomie im 20. Jahrhundert* (Munich, 1970), 47ff.
71 Cf. Marx, *Capital*, vol. 1, 619 (770). A rise in the value of constant capital (for example of raw materials) can equally have consequences which lead towards crisis: it can reduce the proportion of variable capital, i.e. lead to a falling demand for labour (unemployment) and at the same time make the product more expensive (market difficulties). Cf. Marx, *Theories of Surplus Value*, vol. 2, 515f.
72 Cf. Marx, *Theories of Surplus Value*, vol. 2, 517ff, 527ff.
73 Cf. Marx, *Grundrisse*, 149.
74 Marx, *Theories of Surplus Value*, vol. 2, 500.
75 *Ibid*, 503.
76 Cf. here especially Marx, *Capital*, vol. 2, 351ff, 489ff.
77 Cf. ch. 3 of this study.

Chapter 3

1 Cf. F. Lassalle, *Herr Bastiat-Schulze von Delitzsch der ökonomische Julian, oder: Kapital und Arbeit* (1864; reprinted Berlin, 1912).
2 F. Lassalle, *The Working Man's Programme*, translated with an introduction by Edward Peters (London, 1884), 6 (adapted). [Significantly Lassalle uses the term 'Arbeiter*stand*' here, which in German does not have the same connotations of class conflict as the Marxist term 'Arbeiter*klasse*'].
3 Lassalle, *The Working Man's Programme ...*, 54–55.
4 F. Lassalle, 'Offenes Antwortschreiben an das Zentralkommittee zur Berufung eines allgemeinen deutschen Arbeiterkongresses zu Leipzig' (1863), in F. Lassalle, *Reden und Schriften* (Munich, 1970), 170–201. This edition, edited by F. Jenaczek, contains an extensive critical bibliography.
5 *Ibid*, 181.
6 *Ibid*, 188.
7 *Ibid*, 199.
8 Cf. K. Marx, *Critique of the Gotha Programme*, MESW, vol. 3.
9 F. Engels, *A Critique of the Draft Social-Democratic Programme of 1891*, MESW, vol. 3, 432.
10 Particularly important was Karl Kautsky's frequently republished *The Economic Doctrines of Karl Marx* (London, 1925; originally published as *Karl Marx's ökonomische Lehren*, Stuttgart, 1887).
11 K. Kautsky, *Die Agrarfrage. Eine Übersicht über die Tendenzen der modernen Landwirtschaft und die Agrarpolitik der Sozialdemokratie* (Stuttgart, 1899) [cf. also J. Banaji, 'Summary of Selected Parts of Kautsky's "The Agrarian Translation" ', *Economy & Society* 5 (1) (February, 1976), 2–49; Kautsky's study is available in a French translation, *La Question Agraire* (Paris, 1970)].
12 On the definition of revisionism and reformism in this sense cf. W. Hofmann, *Ideengeschichte der sozialen Bewegung des 19. und 20. Jahrhunderts* (Berlin, 1970), 173.
13 Cf. for a detailed discussion B. Gustafsson, *Marxismus und Revisionismus. Eduard Bernstein's Kritik des Marxismus und ihre ideengeschichtlichen Voraussetzungen* (2 vols., Frankfurt, 1972). For the philosophical basis of revisionism cf. also L. Colletti, *Bernstein und der Marxismus der Zweiten Internationale* (Frankfurt, 1971) [cf. also P. Gay, *The Dilemma of Democratic Socialism* (Columbia, 1952)].
14 Cf. Eduard Bernstein, *Evolutionary Socialism: a Criticism and Affirmation* (New

York, 1961; originally published as *Die Voraussetzungen des Sozialismus und die Aufgaben der Sozialdemokratie*, 1899, reprinted Reinbek, 1971). Bernstein's book was preceded by a series of articles in the social democratic journal *Die Neue Zeit*: E. Bernstein, 'Probleme des Sozialismus', *Die Neue Zeit*, 15 (1896/97) & 16 (1897/98). Cf. also E. Bernstein, 'Der Kampf der Sozialdemokratie und die Revolution der Gesellschaft, *Die Neue Zeit* 16 (1897/98).

15 Cf. for an introduction to the concept, Bernstein, *Evolutionary Socialism* ..., 80.
16 *Ibid*, 54.
17 *Ibid*, 99.
18 J. Schumpeter, *History of Economic Analysis* (New York, 1954), 883.
19 R. Luxemburg, *Social Reform or Revolution?* (New York, 1973).
20 K. Kautsky, *Bernstein und das sozialdemokratische Programm: Antikritik* (Stuttgart, 1899).
21 Bernstein, *Evolutionary Socialism* ..., 61.
22 E. Bernstein, 'Entwicklungsgang eines Sozialisten', in F. Meier (ed.), *Die Volkswirtschaftslehre der Gegenwart in Selbstdarstellungen* (Leipzig, 1924), 22.
23 Bernstein, *Evolutionary Socialism* ..., 224.
24 On the Russian revisionism debate cf. Gustafsson, *op. cit.*; R. Kindersley, *The First Russian Revisionists: A Study of Legal Marxism* (Oxford, 1962). The theoretical core of the debate was the 'realization problem' or the 'theory of markets': cf. R. Hickel, 'Zur Interpretation der Marxchen Reproduktionsschemata', *Mehrwert* 2 (May, 1973); R. Rosdolsky, *Entstehungsgeschichte* ..., vol. 2, 524–96; R. Luxemburg, *The Accumulation of Capital* (London, 1951).
25 V. Lenin, *What is to be Done?* CW, 5, 370f.
26 The most important work here is M. Tugan-Baranowsky, *Studien zur Theorie und Geschichte der Handelskrisen in England* (Jena, 1901). This is a translation of the second Russian edition of 1900, the first Russian edition appeared in 1894. For a biography and a study of Tugan-Baranowsky's work as a whole, cf. A. Nove, 'M.T. Tugan-Baranowsky (1865–1919)', *History of Political Economy* 2 (1970), 246–62.
27 Cf. K. Marx, *Capital*, vol. 2, 489–523.
28 M. Tugan-Baranowsky, *Handelskrisen in England* ..., 25.
29 *Ibid*, 31.
30 *Ibid*, Introduction, p. iv.
31 Cf. Nove, *op. cit.*, 247f.
32 Cf. M. Tugan-Baranowsky, *Theoretische Grundlagen des Marxismus* (Leipzig, 1905); idem, *Der moderne Sozialismus in seiner geschichtlichen Entwicklung* (Dresden, 1908); idem, *Soziale Theorie der Verteilung* (Berlin, 1913).
33 Lenin's most important writings on the 'theory of markets' are: V. Lenin, *On the So-Called Market Question* (this manuscript was written in 1893 and discussed in Marxist circles but was only rediscovered and published in 1937) CW, vol. 1; idem, *A Characterization of Economic Romanticism* (1897), CW, vol. 2; idem, *The Development of Capitalism in Russia: The Process of the Formation of a Home Market for Large Scale Industry* (1899), CW, vol. 3.
34 Lenin, *Development of Capitalism* ..., CW, vol. 3, 54f.
35 Luxemburg, *Accumulation of Capital*.
36 V. Lenin, *The Economic Content of Narodism and the Criticism of it in Mr Struve's Book* (1895), CW, vol. 1, 498.
37 V. Lenin, *A Note on the Question of the Market Theory* (1889), CW, vol. 4, 59f.
38 Lenin, *What is to be Done?*, CW, vol. 5, 361.
39 Lenin, *A Note* ..., CW, vol. 4, 62.
40 R. Hilferding, 'Böhm-Bawerk's Criticism of Marx', in P. Sweezy (ed.), *op. cit.*

41 R. Hilferding, *Das Finanzkapital. Eine Studie über die jüngste Entwicklung des Kapitalismus* (1910; Frankfurt and Vienna, 1968), 17.
42 Hilferding, *op. cit.*
43 *Ibid*, 309.
44 *Ibid*, 321f.
45 *Ibid*, 243.
46 *Ibid*, 322.
47 *Ibid*, 503f.
48 Cf. *ibid*, 77 [On Hilferding's Finance Capital cf. A. Hussein, 'Hilferding's Finance Capital', *Bulletin of the Conference of Socialist Economists* 5 (1)(March, 1976)]; W. Gottschalch, *Strukturveränderungen der Gesellschaft und politisches Handeln in der Lehre von Hilferding* (Berlin, 1962); R. Schimkowsky, 'Zur Marx-Rezeption bei Hilferding, Die Bestimmungen von Konkurrenz und Monopol im "Finanzkapital" ', in R. Ebbighausen (ed.), *Monopol und Staat. Zur Marx-Rezeption in der Theorie des staatsmonopolistischen Kapitalismus* (Frankfurt, 1974).
49 Cf. in this sense also Kautsky's judgement that Hilferding's Finance Capital could 'in a certain sense be called a continuation of Marx's "Capital" ', K. Kautsky, 'Finanzkapital und Krisen', *Die Neue Zeit* 29 (1)(1910/1911), 765.
50 Marx, *Capital*, vol. 1, 627ff (779ff).
51 *Ibid*, 628 (780).
52 Marx, *Capital*, vol. 3, 427ff.
53 Engels, *A Critique of the Draft Social Democratic Programme of 1891*, MESW, vol. 3, 432. Cf. also the notes and additions by Engels in Marx, *Capital*, vol. 1, 627 (779) and *Capital*, vol. 3, 428f.
54 Marx, *Capital*, vol. 3, 593f; see also *ibid*, 428.
55 Cf. the explicit reference in Hilferding, *op. cit.*, 333, footnote 5.
56 *Ibid*, 347.
57 M. Tugan-Baranowsky, *Studien zur Theorien und Geschichte der Handelskrise in England* (Jena, 1901), 415.
58 Marx, *Capital*, vol. 2, 107; cf. also Hilferding, *Finanzkapital* ..., 97f, and Lenin, *Notebooks on Imperialism*, CW, vol. 39, 333ff.
59 It is in this sense that for example both Grossmann and Sweezy criticize Hilferding's thesis of the domination of the banks as an invalid generalization of a transitory historical phenomenon; cf. H. Grossmann, *Das Akkumulations- und Zusammenbruchsgesetz des kapitalistischen Systems* (1929; reprinted Frankfurt, 1970), 572ff, and Sweezy, *Theory of Capitalist Development* ..., 266f.
60 Marx, *Capital*, vol. 3, 593ff.
61 Cf. also the Introduction by Eduard März to Hilferding, *Finanzkapital*, 5–16.
62 To a certain extent, Hilferding here falls between two stools: Schumpeter held his theory of money to be a 'rather old fashioned monetary theory', while Lenin criticized precisely his deviation from metallic conceptions. Cf. Schumpeter, *op. cit.*, 881; Lenin, *Notebooks on Imperialism*, CW, vol. 39, 189 & 333; *idem*, *Imperialism: The Highest Stage of Capitalism*, CW, vol. 22.
63 Hilferding, *op. cit.*, 502.
64 *Ibid*, 431.
65 P. Mattick, Postscript to H. Grossmann, *Marx, die klassische Nationalökonomie und das Problem der Dynamik* (Frankfurt and Vienna, 1969), 115.
66 R. Luxemburg, *The Accumulation of Capital* (1913; London, 1947); *idem*, *The Accumulation of Capital: an Anti-Critique* (1915; New York and London, 1972). [This volume also contains Bukharin's *Imperialism and the Accumulation of Capital*, cf. footnote 85 of this chapter].
67 Luxemburg, *Accumulation of Capital*.
68 R. Luxemburg, 'What is Economics' in A. Waters (ed.), *Rosa Luxemburg Speaks* (New York, 1970).

69 Luxemburg, Foreword to *The Accumulation of Capital*.
70 Cf. R. Luxemburg, *Briefe an Leon Jogiches* (Frankfurt, 1971), 356f, and the references to further literature listed there.
71 Eckstein, Gustav, *Rosa Luxemburg. Die Accumulation des Kapitals. Eine Besprechung* (1913), in: Luxemburg, R., *Die Accumulation des Kapitals* (Frankfurt, 1970), 493.
72 O. Bauer, 'Die Akkumulation des Kapitals', *Die Neue Zeit* 31 (1) (1912/13).
73 Cf. A. Pannekoek, 'Theoretisches zur Ursache der Krisen', *Die Neue Zeit* 31 (1912/1913); [cf. also *idem*, 'The Theory of the Collapse of Capitalism' (1934), *Capital and Class* 1 (Spring 1977), 59–81].
74 Lenin, *Letter to L.B. Kamenev* (written before 29.3.1913), CW, vol. 35, 94.
75 Rosdolsky, *Entstehungsgeschichte ...*, 578–596.
76 P. Knirsch, *Die ökonomischen Anschauungen Nikolaj I. Bucharins* (Berlin, 1959). An extensive bibliography by Heitman and Knirsch contains 774 titles written or edited by Bukharin (including the separately listed translations): cf. S. Heitman and P. Knirsch, *N.I. Bucharin* (Bibliographische Mitteilungen des Osteuropa-Instituts an der Freien Universität Berlin, Heft 1 Berlin, 1959); U. Stehr, *Vom Kapitalismus zum Kommunismus, Bukharins Beitrag zur Entwicklung einer sozialistischen Theorie und Gesellschaft* (Düsseldorf, 1973).
77 N. Bukharin, *Die politische Okonomie des Rentners. Die Wert- und Profittheorie der österreichischen Schule* (1919) (Frankfurt, 1966).
78 Cf. P. Knirsch, *Die ökonomische Anschauungen ...*, 7.
79 Cf. N. Bukharin, *Imperialism and World Economy* (1918, reprinted New York, 1973).
80 *Ibid*, 118–119.
81 *Ibid*, 144ff.
82 Cf. K. Kautsky, 'Der Imperialismus', *Die Neue Zeit* 32 (2) (1913/1914).
83 Bukharin, *Imperialism ....*
84 Cf. V. Lenin, 'Introduction' to Bukharin, *Imperialism ....*
85 N. Bukharin, *Ökonomik der Transformationsperiode* (1920) (Reinbek, 1970); N. Bukharin, *Imperialism and the Accumulation of Capital* (ed. K. Tarbuck), (New York and London, 1972).
86 Cf. M. Joelson, 'Monopolistischer Kapitalismus und "organisierter Kapitalismus" ', *Unter dem Banner des Marxismus* 3 (1929).
87 Lenin, 'Introduction' to Bukharin, *Imperialism ...*; also reprinted in CW, vol. 22. The Introduction was written in December 1915.
88 Lenin, 'Introduction', 1of.
89 Lenin, *Imperialism ...*, CW, vol. 22, 266.
90 *Ibid*, 266f.
91 *Ibid*, 195.
92 Cf. Lenin, *Notebooks on Imperialism*, CW, vol. 39.
93 Lenin, *Imperialism ...*, CW, vol. 22, 226.
94 Lenin, 'Introduction', 14.
95 Cf. for a contemporary Marxist-Leninist interpretation of Lenin's theory of imperialism: E. Haak & H. Wunderlich, *Grundkurs zu Lenins Werk 'Der Imperialismus als höchstes Studium des Kapitalismus'* (Berlin, 1971). A criticism of Lenin's theory of imperialism which appeals to Marx's arguments is provided by C. Neusüss, *Imperialismus und Weltmarktbewegung des Kapitals* (Erlangen, 1972); also D. Jordan, 'Der Imperialismus als monopolistischer Kapitalismus: Zur Imperialismus-Analyse Lenins als Basis der Theorie des staatsmonopolistischen Kapitalismus', in R. Ebbighausen (ed.), *Monopol und Staat ....*
96 Lenin, *Imperialism ...*, CW, vol. 22, 189.
97 *Ibid*, 298.
98 V. Lenin, *State and Revolution: The Marxist Teaching on the State and the Task of the Proletariat in the Revolution*, CW, vol. 25, 383, 410.

99 *Ibid*, 383.
100 Cf. V. Lenin, *The Impending Catastrophe and How to Combat it*, CW, vol. 25, 358 (emphasis in the original).
101 For a positive position, cf. Autorenkollektiv, *Politische Ökonomie des heutigen Monopolkapitalismus* (Frankfurt, 1972), 10; S. Wygodski, *Der gegenwärtige Kapitalismus. Versuch einer theoretischen Analyse* (Cologne, 1972). An opposing position is provided by M. Wirth, *Kapitalismustheorie in der DDR Entstehung und Entwicklung der Theorie des staatsmonopolistischen Kapitalismus* (Frankfurt, 1972), 21–4.
102 Institut für Gesellschaftswissenschaften beim ZK der SED (ed.), *Der Imperialismus der BRD* (Frankfurt, 1972), 6.

Chapter 4

1 First Congress of the Communist International, Moscow March 2nd to March 10th 1919, *Protocol* (German edition, Hamburg, 1921), 171.
2 *Ibid*, 174.
3 *Ibid*.
4 Cf. E. Varga, *Die Krise der Kapitalistischen Weltwirtschaft* (Hamburg, 1921).
5 *Ibid*, 60. Cf. also E. Varga, *The Decline of Capitalism* (London, 1928).
6 Fifth World Congress of the Communist International, Moscow, June 17th to July 8th 1924 *Theses and Resolutions* (German edition, Hamburg, 1924), 37.
7 Cf. E. Varga, *Aufstieg oder Niedergang des Kapitalismus* (Hamburg, 1924); Fifth Meeting of the Expanded Executive of the Communist International, Moscow March 21st to April 6th 1925, *Protocol* (German edition, Hamburg, 1925). The political context of the thesis of 'relative stabilization' is examined in detail by H. Heilmann & B. Rabehl, 'Die Legende von der "Bolschewisierung" der KPD', *Sozialistische Politik* 9 (December, 1970).
8 *Internationale Pressekorrespondenz* 5 (21) (5.2.1925), 269f. Cited here according to E. Varga, *Die Krise des Kapitalismus und die politischen Folgen*, ed. E. Altvater (Frankfurt and Vienna, 1969), xvi. Cf. also E. Varga, *The Decline of Capitalism: The Economics of a Period of the Decline of Capitalism after Stabilization* (London, 1928).
9 Cf. N. Bukharin, *Die kapitalistische Stabilisierung und die proletarische Revolution* (Report to the Seventh Expanded Plenum of the Executive Committee of the Comintern; Moscow, 1926), 4ff.
10 Cf. E. Varga, *The Decline of Capitalism: The Economics of a Period of the Decline of Capitalism after Stabilization* (London, 1928). Cf. also the summary in M. Wirth, *Kapitalismustheorie in der DDR. Entwicklung und Entstehung der Theorie des staatsmonopolistischen Kapitalismus* (Frankfurt, 1972), 23ff. The same idea, but without the term state capitalism, can be found already in F. Engels, *Socialism: Utopian and Scientific*, MESW, 3, 144f; idem, *Anti-Dühring*, 384f.
11 Cf. E. Varga, *The Great Crisis and its Political Consequences: Economics and Politics 1928–1934* (London, 1935), 68–9. Partially reprinted in E. Altvater, *op. cit.*
12 Varga, *The Great Crisis ...*, 69.
13 Cf. the Introduction by Altvater in Altvater, *op. cit.*, ix–xxxix. This volume also reprints excerpts from Varga's economic analyses of the period.
14 For an overview of German economic analysis of the period, cf. for example H. Kuschmann, *Die Untersuchungen des Instituts für Konjunkturforschung* (Jena, 1933).
15 R. Hilferding, *Das Finanzkapital* (1910; Frankfurt and Vienna, 1968), 20.
16 On social democratic economic policy between the wars cf. *inter alia* C. Kindelberger, *The World in Depression, 1929–1939* (History of the World Economy in the Twentieth Century vol. 4, London, 1973); H. Arndt, *The Economic Lessons of the 1930s* (London, 1944); R. Skidelsky, *Politicians and the Slump: The Labour Government of 1929–1931* (Harmondsworth, 1970).

17 Cf. the detailed study by W. Gottschalch, *Strukturveränderungen der Gesellschaft und politisches Handeln in der Lehre von Hilferding* (Berlin, 1962); R. Schimkowsky, 'Exkurs über Hilferding: vom Generalkartell zur Konzeption des organisierten Kapitalismus' in R. Ebbighausen (ed.), *Monopol und Staat. Zur Marx-Rezeption in der Theorie des staatsmonopolistischen Kapitalismus* (Frankfurt, 1974); H. Winkler, 'Einleitende Bermerkungen zu Hilferding's Theorie des Organisierten Kapitalismus' in Winkler (ed.), *Organisierter Kapitalismus, Voraussetzungen und Anfänge* (Göttingen, 1974).

18 Cf. G. Hardach, 'Französische Rüstungspolitik 1914–1918', in Winkler (ed.), *op. cit.*, 109ff.

19 There are some parallels between Hilferding's 'organized capitalism' and Bukharin's 'state capitalism', even though the two theories have different political consequences. Cf. M. Joelson, 'Monopolistischer Kapitalismus und "organisierter" Kapitalismus', *Unter dem Banner des Marxismus* 3 (1929).

20 R. Hilferding, 'Arbeitsgemeinschaft der Klassen?' *Der Kampf* 8 (1915), 322, cited according to W. Gottschalch, *Strukturveränderungen ..., op. cit.*, 190. Cf. also *idem, Die Sozialisierung und die Machtverhältnisse der Klassen* (speech at the 1st Congress of Workers' Councils given on 5 October 1920: Berlin, 1920).

21 R. Hilferding, 'Probleme der Zeit', *Die Gesellschaft* 1 (1924).

22 *Idem, Die Aufgaben der Sozialdemokratie in der Republik* (speech at the SPD Congress in Kiel, 1927; Berlin, 1927), 168.

23 The chief work is F. Naphtali, *Wirtschaftsdemokratie* (1928; Frankfurt, 1968). For a critical discussion cf. above all D. Schneider and R. Kuda, *Mitbestimmung* (Munich, 1969).

24 Allgemeiner Kongress der Arbeiter- und Soldatenräte Deutschlands vom 16. bis 21. Dezember im Abgeordnetenhaus zu Berlin. Stenographische Berichte (Berlin, 1919), 312–44.

25 Cf. R. Hilferding, 'Probleme der Zeit', *op. cit.*, 2; *idem, Gesellschaftsmacht oder Privatmacht über die Wirtschaft*, Referat auf dem 4. AFA-Gewerksschaftskongress, Leipzig vom 5.–7. Oktober 1931 (Berlin, 1931); W. Gottschalch, *op. cit.*, 196; Winkler, 'Einleitende Bemerkungen ...', *op. cit.*, 13.

26 Cf. the various arguments in Winkler (ed.), *op. cit.*

27 Stenographischer Bericht der Verhandlungen des Vereins für Sozialpolitik in Wien 1926 (*Schriften des Vereins für Sozialpolitik*, vol. 172; Munich and Leipzig, 1926), 113f. At the end of the quoted passage the protocol reports 'Laughter and calls of "quite right" '.

28 N. Bukharin, *Imperialism and the Accumulation of Capital* (1925/26), (London and New York, 1972).

29 *Ibid*, 226ff.

30 Recently J. Glombowski has developed a general form of the reproduction schema: J. Glombowski, 'Gleichgewichtige erweiterte Reproduktion mit variablen Wachstumsraten der Kapitale', *Mehrwert* 2 (May, 1973), 110–122.

31 F. Sternberg, *Der Imperialismus* (1926; Frankfurt, 1971), 88.

32 *Ibid*, 47, 591.

33 *Ibid*, 355.

34 For criticism cf. J. Goldstein, 'Fritz Sternbergs "Imperialismus" ', *Unter dem Banner des Marxismus* 4 (1930); H. Grossmann, 'Eine neue Theorie über Imperialismus und die soziale Revolution', *Archiv für die Geschichte des Sozialismus und der Arbeiterbewegung* (Grünbergs Archiv) 13 (1928). Sternberg's own extensive reply to his critics contains no new arguments, cf. F. Sternberg, *'Der Imperialismus' und seine Kritiker* (Berlin, 1929).

35 F. Sternberg, *Der Niedergang des deutschen Kapitalismus* (Berlin, 1932); *idem, The Coming Crisis* (London, 1927) [discussed in Appendix III of K. Tarbuck (ed.). *The Accumulation of Capital* (New York and London, 1972), 278–280]; F. Sternberg, *Kapitalismus und Sozialismus vor dem Weltgericht* (Hamburg, 1952).

36 H. Grossmann, *Das Akkumulations- und Zusammenbruchsgesetz des kapitalistischen Systems* (1929; Frankfurt 1970), 178. The new edition of Grossmann's book contains a bibliography of his writings and of the literature on his work. For a detailed discussion cf. the dissertation by M. Trottmann, *Zur Interpretation und Kritik der Zusammenbruchstheorie von Henryk Grossmann* (Zurich, 1956).

37 O. Bauer, 'Die Akkumulation des Kapitals', *Die Neue Zeit* 31 (1912/1913); cf. also the discussion in P.M. Sweezy, *The Theory of Capitalist Development: Principles of Marxian Political Economy* (New York, 1949), 210f.

38 Sweezy, *Capitalist Development* ..., 210.

39 Cf. H. Grossmann, *Akkumulations- und Zusammenbruchsgesetz* ..., 195f. Marx, *Capital*, vol. 3, 214.

40 Sweezy, *Capitalist Development* ..., 211.

41 Cf. also M. Trottmann, *op. cit.*, 83.

42 Naturally for the Communist International this was particularly irritating, cf. E. Varga, 'Akkumulation und Zusammenbruch des Kapitalismus', *Unter dem Banner des Marxismus* 4 (1930).

43 N. Moskowszka, *Zur Kritik moderner Krisentheorien* (Prague, 1935); Sweezy, *Capitalist Development* ...

44 On 'neomarxism' as it is used here cf. the collection of essays by P. Mattick, *Kritik der Neomarxisten und andere Aufsätze* (Frankfurt, 1974).

45 P. Sweezy, *op. cit.*

46 Cf. *ibid*, 183ff.

47 *Ibid*, 274.

48 P. Baran and P. Sweezy, *Monopoly Capital: An Essay on the American Economic and Political Order* (Harmondsworth, 1968).

49 *Ibid*, 21.

50 P. Baran, *The Political Economy of Growth* (Harmondsworth, 1973). Emphasis in the original.

51 Baran and Sweezy, *Monopoly Capital* ... , 23.

52 For a critical discussion of *Monopoly Capital* cf. *inter alia*, F. Hermania, K. Monte and C. Rolshausen (eds.), *Monopolkapital. Thesen zu dem Buch von Paul A. Baran and Paul M. Sweezy* (Frankfurt, 1973).

53 There is a striking parallel here to the widespread popularity in the 1960s of Marcuse's adaptation of Marx, cf. H. Marcuse, *One-Dimensional Man* (London, 1964).

54 In this sense an important stage was the delayed reception in West Germany of Mandel's book: E. Mandel, *Marxist Economic Theory* (1962, London, 1968).

55 J. Stalin, *Economic Problems of Socialism in the USSR*. Cf. also, J. Stalin, J. Behrens, F. Kuczynski, *Ökonomische Probleme des Sozialismus* (Frankfurt, 1972). The writings collected in this volume by the 'Roter Druckstock' include, as well as Stalin's study itself, some contemporary commentaries on what Behrens terms 'this work of genius'.

56 Lenin, *Imperialism* ..., CW, vol. 22.

57 Stalin, *op. cit.*

58 E. Varga, *Grundfragen der Ökonomie und Politik des Imperialismus nach dem zweiten Weltkrieg* (Berlin, 1955).

59 *Ibid*, 115.

60 Cf. J. Schmidt, *Neue Probleme der Krisentheorie* (Berlin, 1956); R. Ründel, *Die zyklische Entwicklung der westdeutschen Wirtschaft von 1950–1957* (Berlin, 1957); E. Varga, 'Probleme des industriellen Nachkriegszyklus und die neue Überproduktionskrise' *Sowjetwissenschaft* 12 (1958); H. Heininger, *Der Nachkriegszyklus der westdeutschen Wirtschaft 1945–1950* (Berlin, 1959).

61 Cf. W. Petrowsky, 'Zur Entwicklung der Theorie des staatsmonopolistischen Kapitalismus', *Probleme des Klassenkampfes* 1 (1971), 141.

62 K. Zieschang, 'Zu einigen theoretischen Problemen des staatsmonopolistischen Kapitalismus', *Wirtschaftswissenschaft* 4 (1956); *idem*, 'Zu einigen theoretischen Problem des staatsmonopolistischen Kapitalismus in Westdeutschland', *Probleme der politischen Ökonomie, Jahrbuch des Instituts für Wirtschaftswissenschaften der Deutschen Akademie der Wissenschaften zu Berlin* 1 (1957). For a detailed discussion of the development of 'stamocap' theory in the GDR cf. M. Wirth, *Kapitalismustheorie in der DDR. Entstehung und Entwicklung der Theorie des staatsmonopolistischen Kapitalismus* (Frankfurt, 1972).

63 As an exception cf. P. Lapinski, 'Der "Sozialstaat". Etappen und Tendenzen seiner Entwicklung', *Unter dem Banner des Marxismus* 2 (1928).

64 *Diskussion über das Buch 'Veränderungen in der kapitalistischen Wirtschaft im Gefolge des zweiten Weltkriegs' von E. Varga* (1st supplement to *Sowjetwissenschaft*, Berlin, 1947), 12ff.

65 *Ibid*, 14.

66 Cf. Wirth, *op. cit.*, 26.

67 This applies to the development of the theory in the GDR, cf. Wirth, *op. cit.*, 62ff, and Petrowsky, *op. cit.*, 145. The development of the theory outside the GDR has still to be systematically investigated.

68 Three recent studies from the GDR, the USSR and France and presented in Institut für Marxistische Studien und Forschungen (ed.), *Der staatsmonopolistische Kapitalismus. Einführung in marxistische Analysen aus der DDR, Frankreich und der Sowjetunion* (Frankfurt, 1972). Particularly valuable as an introduction to the theoretical position is R. Katzenstein, 'Zur Theorie des staatsmonopolistischen Kapitalismus', *Probleme des Klassenkampfes* 3 (1973).

69 Autorenkollektiv, *Politische Ökonomie des heutigen Monopolkapitalismus* (Frankfurt, 1970).

70 S. Wygodski, *Der gegenwärtige Kapitalismus. Versuch einter theoretischen Analyse* (Cologne, 1972).

71 *Lehrbuch Politische Ökonomie. Vorsozialistische Produktionsweisen* (Frankfurt, 1972).

72 R. Gündel, H. Heininger, P. Hess, K. Zieschang, *Zur Theorie des staatsmonopolistischen Kapitalismus* (Berlin, 1967).

73 Autorenkollektiv, *Imperialismus heute. Der staatsmonopolistische Kapitalismus in Westdeutschland* (Berlin, 1965). A continuation of this argument has appeared as Autorenkollektiv, *Der Imperialismus in der BRD* (Frankfurt, 1972).

74 Autorenkollektiv, *Der staatsmonopolistische Kapitalismus* (Frankfurt, 1972).

75 Autorenkollektiv, *Imperialismus in der BRD ...*, 606.

76 Autorenkollektiv, *Der staatsmonopolistische Kapitalismus ...*, 648.

77 Cf. *ibid*, 24ff.

78 *Lehrbuch Politische Ökonomie ...*, 552f.

79 This is the direction of the criticism *inter alia* of E. Mandel, *Der Spätkapitalismus. Versuch einer marxistischen Erklärung* (Frankfurt, 1972), 485ff; W. Petrowsky, *op. cit.*; W. Müller and C. Neusüss, 'The Illusion of State Socialism and the Contradiction between Wage Labour and Capital' *Telos* 25 (Fall, 1975).

80 Cf. at length M. Wirth, *op. cit.* Further contributions (of varying quality) to the discussion are continually appearing, cf. *inter alia*, R. Ebbighausen (ed.), *Monopol und Staat. Zur Marx-Rezeption in der Theorie des staatsmonopolistischen Kapitalismus* (Frankfurt, 1974); J. Schubert, 'Die Theorie des staatsmonopolistischen Kapitalismus' *Mehrwert* 4 (September, 1973); M. Wirth, 'Zur Kritik des staatsmonopolistischen Kapitalismus', *Probleme des Klassenkampfes* 3 (1973).

81 A preliminary presentation of the stages of the history of the theory is contained in M. Wirth, *Kapitalismustheorie ...*, 21ff.

82 Cf. Autorenkollektiv, *Imperialismus der BRD ...*, 614.

Chapter 5

1 Represented, for example, at its most sophisticated by I. Steedman, *Marx after Sraffa,* New Left Books, London, 1977, which contains references to much of the literature.
2 See page 25 above.
3 Because the necessary *mathematical* amendments are easily made (although *interpretation* of the solutions are not so easily decided). See F. Seton, 'The "Transformation Problem" ', *Review of Economic Studies,* 24, 1957.
4 See, for example, G. Pilling, 'The Law of Value in Ricardo and Marx', *Economy and Society*1,3, August 1972.
5 See p. 19.
6 W. Baumol, 'The Transformation Problem: What Marx Really Meant', *Journal of Economic Literature,* March 1974.
7 I. Gerstein, 'Production, Circulation and Value: The Significance of the "Transformation Problem" in Marx's Critique of Political Economy', *Economy and Society,* 1976.
8 B. Fine and L. Harris, 'Controversial Issues in Marxist Economic Theory', *The Socialist Register,* 1976, edited by R. Miliband and J. Saville.
9 Analysed by Marx in Volume II of *Capital.* See also B. Fine 'The Circulation of Capital, Ideology and Crisis', *Bulletin of the Conference of Socialist Economists* IV. 12, October 1975.
10 B. Rowthorn, 'Vulgar Economy', *Bulletin of the Conference of Socialist Economists* II. 5, Spring 1973, reprinted in *New Left Review* 84, 1974.
11 For example, D. Yaffe 'Value and Price in Marx's *Capital*', *Revolutionary Communist 1,* January 1975.
12 G. Hodgson, 'Papering Over the Cracks', *Socialist Register 1977,* edited by R. Miliband and J. Saville, B. Fine and L. Harris *op. cit.* and 'Surveying The Foundations', *Socialist Register 1977.*
13 According to the method sketched out on p. 18.
14 For a characterization and criticism of which at a simple level, see *Economics: An Anti-Text,* edited by F. Green and P. Nore, Macmillan, 1976.
15 P. Sraffa, *Production of Commodities by Means of Commodities* Cambridge, 1960. J. Robinson, 'The Production Function and the Theory of Capital', *Review of Economic Studies,* 1953–54.
16 For a survey and extension of these arguments, see G. C. Harcourt, *Some Cambridge Controversies in the Theory of Capital,* Cambridge, 1972.
17 See B. Fine and L. Harris, 'Surveying the Foundations', *op. cit.*
18 Most notably P. A. Samuelson.
19 See pages 25–7.
20 See page 27 above.
21 See, in particular, G. Hodgson, 'The Theory of the Falling Rate of Profit'. *New Left Review* 84, 1974.
22 See, in particular, D. Yaffe, 'The Marxian Theory of Crisis, Capital and the State', *Economy and Society* 2.2, 1973.
23 See Chapter 4, Section 4. For a survey of underconsumptionist theories, see M. Bleaney *Underconsumptionist Theories,* Cambridge University Press.
24 See for example, the essays collected in H. Magdoff and P. Sweezy, *The End of Prosperity: The American Economy in the 1970s,* New York, 1977.
25 A. Glyn and R. B. Sutcliffe, *British Capitalism, Workers and the Profit Squeeze,* Penguin Books, 1972. It may be argued that for a particular sector, increased competition (temporarily) squeezes profit margins, but this cannot be generalized to the economy as a whole. For then capitalists benefit from the competition in the sectors from which they purchase inputs.
26 See D. Bullock and D. Yaffe, 'Inflation, Crisis and the Post-War Boom'. *Revolutionary Communist,* 3/4, November 1975.
27 E. Mandel, *Late Capitalism,* New Left Books, 1976 B. Rowthorn 'Late Capitalism: A Review Article', *New Left Review* 98, 1976.

28 See works cited for theoretical analysis and B. Fine and L. Harris, 'The British Economy since March 1974' and '...: May 1975–January 1976' *Bulletin of the Conference of Socialist Economists,* October 1975 and June 1976 for conjunctural analyses.

29 See I. Gough 'State Expenditure in Advanced Capitalism', *New Life Review,* 92, 1975.

30 See B. Fine and L. Harris, 'State Expenditure in Advanced Capitalism: A Critique', *New Left Review,* 98, 1976.

31 We cannot survey the debate on this here. See B. Fine and L. Harris, 'Controversial Issues ...' *op. cit.*

32 L. Althusser and E. Balibar, *Reading Capital,* New Left Books, 1970. N. Poulantzas *Political Power and Social Class,* New Left Books, 1973, and *Classes in Contemporary Capitalism,* New Left Books, 1975.

33 For a survey of contributions see B. Jessop, 'Recent Theories of the Capitalist State', *Cambridge Journal of Economics,* December, 1977.

34 See C. Palloix, 'The Internationalization of Capital and the Circuit of Social Capital' in H. Radice (ed.), *International Firms and Modern Imperialism,* Penguin, 1975.

35 R. Murray, 'The Internationalizations of Capital and the Nation State', *New Left Review* 67, 1971.

36 See, for example, Mandel *op. cit.* and Bullock and Yaffe *op. cit.*

37 This is not to suggest that the Keynesian mode of analysis is appropriate for earlier periods of capitalism.

38 For a survey of contributions to an analysis of the E.E.C., see J. Holloway, 'Some Issues Raised by Marxist Analyses of European Integration', *Bulletin of the Conference of Socialist Economists,* 1976.

39 See works already cited.

40 A. G. Frank, *Lumpenbourgeoisie: Lumpendevelopment,* New York, 1972 for example and A. Emmanuel, *Unequal Exchange,* New Left Books, 1972.

41 See E. Laclau, 'Feudalism and Capitalism in Latin America', *New Left Review* 67, 1971 and C. Bettelheim in *Unequal Exchange, op. cit.*

42 See Laclau and also R. Brenner, 'The Origins of Capitalist Development: A Critique of Neo-Smithian Marxism', *New Left Review* 104, 1977 for an historical and theoretical critique of unequal exchange.

43 See Brenner.

44 It should be remembered that the interests of international capital are not fixed historically (maximizing surplus appropriated from a colony for example) nor even if they were would they assume the same form. As we have seen, capital is increasingly internationalized currently in the process of production itself and this is reflected in the location of production plants in the periphery coordinated with those in the metropolis.

Further Reading

The best approach to early socialist theory is through accounts of the development of the working class movement itself: for England E. P. Thompson's *The Making of the English Working Class* (Harmondsworth, Penguin, 1968) remains invaluable, while J. Foster, *Class Struggle and the Industrial Revolution* (London, Weidenfeld and Nicolson, 1974) provides a more recent and focused account. On Marx himself there is no substitute for reading *Capital* itself, in particular Volume I. If it is possible, this is best done with other people in a reading and discussion group – '*Capital* reading groups' have often proved to be an exciting and politically relevant introduction to Marx's work. An account of the relationship of *Capital* to Marx's theoretical development is given in Ernest Mandel, *The Formation of the Economic Thought of Karl Marx* (London, New Left Books), while Ben Fine's *Marx's Capital* (London, Macmillan, 1977) is a brief and useful study of *Capital* as a whole. German revisionism is best tackled through its leading opponent, Rosa Luxemburg, the subject of Norman Geras's *The Legacy of Rosa Luxemburg* (London, New Left Books, 1976). Contemporary Marxist discussion increasingly involves two rather new areas, that of the labour process itself and that of the capitalist state: here the decisive works are undoubtedly for the former H. Braverman, *Labor and Monopoly Capital* (London, Monthly Review Press, 1974), and for the latter, Nicos Poulantzas, *Classes in Contemporary Capitalism* (London, New Left Books, 1975).

Name Index

Subject Index